Catholic Healing the Inner Child

A Comprehensive Recovery Workbook to
Overcome past Trauma and Experience
Inner Wholeness through Meditations and
Spiritual Exercises

By

Margaret Anne Walsh

Disclaimer notice

Please be aware that the information provided in this document is intended solely for educational and entertainment purposes. Every effort has been made to ensure the content is accurate, reliable, current, and complete.

However, no guarantees, either explicit or implicit, are made. Readers acknowledge that the author is not providing legal, financial, medical, or professional advice.

The content has been sourced from various references. It is strongly recommended that you consult a licensed professional before attempting any of the of the methods described in this document.

By reading this document, you agree that the author is not liable for any direct or indirect losses resulting from the use of the information within, including but not limited to errors, omissions, or inaccuracies.

Table of Contents

Introduction

Hey there, fellow seeker of healing and wholeness! Have you ever felt like a part of you is still stuck in the past, carrying wounds from childhood that seem to hold you back in your adult life? Well, you're not alone. That's precisely why I decided to write this book.

Like many of you, I found myself grappling with painful memories and emotional baggage from my past, wondering how to break free from the patterns that seemed to keep repeating themselves in my life.

Growing up in a Catholic family, I was taught the importance of faith, prayer, and forgiveness. But it wasn't until I delved deeper into my Catholic faith that I discovered a profound source of healing for my 'inner child ', a term used to describe the wounded, vulnerable parts of ourselves that we carry from childhood. Drawing on the rich traditions of Catholic spirituality,

I began to explore how Christ's teachings and the Church's wisdom could offer solace and transformation to those wounded parts of myself.

In this book, I invite you to embark on a journey of healing and self-discovery through the lens of Catholic spirituality.

Together, we'll explore how faith, love, and redemption principles can illuminate the path to healing our inner child and reclaiming our true identity as beloved children of God.

Throughout the pages of this book, you'll find a blend of personal reflections, scriptural insights, and practical exercises designed to guide you on your healing journey.

We'll start by understanding the wounds of our inner child, then move on to exploring forgiveness, self-compassion, and inner peace. We'll draw on the timeless wisdom of Catholic saints and mystics to illuminate our path forward.

This book is not just about theory or theology, but about real-life transformation. As we journey together, you will uncover practical tools and strategies that will help you release old wounds, cultivate a deeper self-love, and embrace the fullness of life that God desires for you.

By the time you reach the end of this book, I hope you'll have a deeper understanding of your inner child and the wounds that need healing and a renewed sense of hope and purpose.

So, are you ready to embark on this journey of healing and transformation? Your active participation is crucial in this process. If so, let's dive in together and discover the profound healing power of Catholic spirituality for your inner child. It's time to reclaim your true identity and embrace the abundant life that awaits you!

Chapter 1: Embarking on a journey of self-discovery

1.1 The importance of self-help in modern life

In the context of our fast-paced, technology-driven world, self-help has emerged as a vital tool. The 21st century presents us with a myriad of challenges, many of which are unprecedented. The rapid advancement of technology, the escalating demands of the workplace, and the constant influx of information have all contributed to a surge in stress and anxiety levels. In this landscape, self-help practices are not just beneficial, but they have become a necessity for maintaining our mental and emotional well-being.

Rapid changes and significant pressures mark the modern era. With the advent of social media, we are constantly exposed to other people's lives, often leading to feelings of inadequacy and self-doubt. The workplace has also evolved, with many individuals juggling multiple roles and responsibilities.

This can lead to burnout, a condition characterized by extreme physical and mental exhaustion. In such a scenario, self-help offers practical solutions to manage stress, improve mental health, and enhance overall quality of life.

One of the primary benefits of self-help is its ability to promote self-awareness. By engaging in self-reflection and mindfulness practices, individuals can better understand their thoughts, emotions, and behaviors. This increased awareness allows them to identify areas that need improvement and take proactive steps to address them. For example, mindfulness meditation can help reduce stress and improve focus, while journaling can provide insights into personal patterns and triggers.

Self-help also empowers individuals to take control of their lives. Self-help encourages people to look within themselves rather than relying on external sources for validation or solutions. This shift in perspective can lead to greater self-confidence and resilience. When individuals feel empowered, they are more likely to set and achieve personal goals, which fosters a sense of accomplishment and satisfaction.

Moreover, self-help practices can lead to improved relationships. Individuals often become better communicators and more empathetic towards others by working on themselves. This can enhance their interactions with family, friends, and colleagues. Techniques such as active listening and assertiveness training can help individuals express their needs more clearly and understand others' perspectives, leading to healthier and more fulfilling relationships.

In addition to personal benefits, self-help has a broader social impact. Individuals becoming more self-aware and emotionally balanced are better equipped to contribute positively to their communities. This can lead to a more supportive and compassionate society. Self-help practices such as volunteering and community engagement can further enhance this positive ripple effect, promoting a sense of belonging and collective well-being.

The importance of self-help in modern life cannot be overstated. As we navigate an increasingly complex and demanding world, self-help offers valuable tools for managing stress, enhancing self-awareness, and improving overall well-being. By empowering individuals to take control of their lives and fostering healthier relationships, self-help benefits the individual and contributes to a more positive and connected society. Embracing self-help practices is crucial to achieving a balanced and fulfilling life in the modern era.

1.2 The Christian perspective on self-help

In the Christian faith, self-help is viewed through God's love and guidance. While "self-help" may seem focused on individual efforts, Christians believe that true healing and growth come from a partnership between the individual and God. This perspective emphasizes the importance of seeking God's will and relying on His strength to overcome challenges and achieve personal transformation.

At the core of the Christian perspective on self-help is the belief in God's unconditional love and grace. Christians believe that God cares deeply for each person and desires their well-being. This love serves as a foundation for self-help efforts, assuring individuals that they are not alone in their struggles. By aligning themselves with God's love, Christians can find strength and courage to face adversity and pursue personal growth.

Central to the Christian faith is the concept of redemption and forgiveness. Christians believe that through the sacrifice of Jesus Christ, they are offered forgiveness for their sins and the opportunity for new life. This belief shapes the way Christians approach self-help, as they recognize their need for healing and restoration. Instead of relying solely on their own efforts, Christians turn to God for forgiveness, guidance, and transformation.

Prayer is a fundamental aspect of the Christian perspective on self-help. Christians believe in the power of prayer to connect with God and seek His intervention in their lives. Through prayer, individuals can express their needs, fears, and desires to God, trusting that He hears and responds to their prayers. Prayer is not only a means of asking for help but also a way of deepening one's relationship with God and aligning oneself with His will.

Scripture plays a vital role in the Christian approach to self-help. The Bible is God's Word and contains teachings and stories that offer wisdom, encouragement, and guidance for daily living. Christians turn to the Bible for inspiration, comfort, and direction in their self-help journey. The stories of faith heroes like David, Esther, and Paul exemplify God's faithfulness and the transformative power of His love.

Christian self-help also emphasizes the importance of community and fellowship. Christians believe they are part of the body of Christ, a community of believers united by their faith in Jesus Christ. This sense of belonging provides support, accountability, and encouragement for individuals on their self-help journey. Through fellowship with other believers, Christians can share their struggles, celebrate victories, and grow together in faith.

The Christian perspective on self-help believes that true healing and transformation come from God. While individuals are called to take responsibility for their actions and choices, they do so in partnership with God, relying on His strength, wisdom, and grace. By embracing God's love, seeking His guidance through prayer and Scripture, and participating in the community of faith, Christians can experience profound growth and healing in their lives.

1.3 Goal setting for personal transformation

Setting goals is an essential step in the journey of personal transformation. Goals provide direction, motivation, and a sense of purpose, guiding individuals toward desired changes. In the context of self-help, setting goals involves identifying areas for improvement, envisioning the desired outcome, and creating a plan to achieve it.

1) Identifying Areas for Improvement

The first step in setting goals for personal transformation is to identify areas of life that require attention. This could include physical health, emotional well-being, relationships, career, spirituality, or personal development. By reflecting on one's current circumstances and considering where growth is needed, individuals can gain clarity on the areas they want to focus on.

2) Envisioning the Desired Outcome

Once areas for improvement have been identified, it's essential to envision the desired outcome. This involves imagining success in each region and setting specific, measurable goals that align with this vision. For example, if the goal is to improve physical health, the desired outcome might be to lose a certain amount of weight, improve endurance, or adopt healthier eating habits.

3) Creating a Plan

With the desired outcome in mind, individuals can create a plan to achieve their goals. This plan should include actionable steps, timelines, and resources needed to support progress. Breaking down larger goals into smaller, manageable tasks can make the process more achievable and reduce overwhelming feelings. It's also helpful to anticipate potential obstacles and develop strategies for overcoming them.

4) Tracking Progress

Monitoring progress is crucial for staying on track and maintaining motivation. Reviewing goals, tracking activities, and celebrating milestones can help individuals stay focused and inspired. Keeping a journal, using a goal-tracking app, or seeking accountability from a friend or mentor are effective ways to track progress and remain committed to personal transformation.

5) Adjusting as Needed

It's essential to recognize that personal transformation is a dynamic process that may require adjustments. As individuals progress toward their goals, they may encounter new challenges, reassess priorities, or discover different paths to success. Flexibility and openness to change allow individuals to adapt their objectives and strategies as needed, ensuring continued growth and progress.

By setting clear goals, envisioning the desired outcome, creating a plan, tracking progress, and remaining flexible, individuals can embark on a journey of personal transformation with confidence and determination. With commitment, perseverance, and support from others, they can overcome obstacles, achieve their goals, and experience meaningful change in their lives.

Chapter 2: Knowing and understanding the inner child

2.1 Acknowledging the inner child

Understanding the concept of the inner child is like discovering a hidden treasure within yourself. Just as a tree's roots anchor and sustain it, our inner child represents the roots of our emotional and psychological well-being. But what exactly is this inner child?

Think back to when you were a child. Remember the innocence, the wonder, and the joy of discovery? That's your inner child. It's the part of you that experienced life with unfiltered authenticity, free from the burdens and responsibilities of adulthood. However, it's not just the joyful memories that define the inner child; it also encompasses the wounds, fears, and unmet needs from childhood.

Our childhood experiences shape who we are as adults. Positive experiences contribute to our emotional resilience and self-esteem, while negative experiences can leave emotional scars that influence our behavior and relationships. These experiences become ingrained in our inner child, affecting how we perceive ourselves, others, and the world around us.

Understanding our inner child is not just a journey, it's a transformative adventure. It's like shining a light into the darkest corners of our psyche, bringing awareness to unconscious patterns and beliefs that drive our thoughts, emotions, and actions. By reconnecting with our inner child, we can not only heal past wounds and overcome limiting beliefs but also cultivate a deeper sense of self-compassion and acceptance, paving the way for a more fulfilling and authentic life.

But how do we begin this journey of self-discovery and healing? It starts with acknowledging the existence of our inner child and honoring its presence in our lives. This involves developing self-awareness and tuning into our emotions, thoughts, and behaviors with curiosity and compassion.

As we explore our inner child, we may uncover painful memories or emotions buried deep within us. These may include experiences of neglect, rejection, abandonment, or trauma. While facing these emotions can be daunting, it's an essential step toward healing. By acknowledging and validating our inner child's pain, we can release trapped emotions and begin the process of healing and integration.

Moreover, understanding our inner child can provide valuable insights into our present-day struggles and challenges. Many of the patterns and behaviors we exhibit as adults are rooted in our childhood experiences. By identifying these patterns, we can clarify why we react a certain way in certain situations and take steps to break free from unhealthy patterns.

Embracing our inner child is not just an act of self-love, it's a profound act of self-compassion. It's about accepting ourselves fully, including the wounded parts that we may have been conditioned to reject or suppress. By nurturing our inner child with love, understanding, and acceptance, we cannot only heal but also transform our lives, offering ourselves the compassion and support we may have longed for in the past.

2.2 The impact of childhood experiences

Our childhood experiences have a profound influence on who we become as adults. The interactions, relationships, and environments we encounter during our formative years significantly shape our beliefs, behaviors, and emotions. Here's how childhood experiences impact our inner child:

Formation of core beliefs

During childhood, we develop core beliefs about ourselves, others, and the world around us. These beliefs are often formed based on our early interactions with caregivers, peers, and authority figures. Positive experiences, such as receiving love and validation, can lead to healthy beliefs about worthiness and self-esteem. Conversely, negative experiences, such as criticism or neglect, can lead to beliefs of unworthiness, inadequacy, or unlovability.

Development of coping mechanisms

In response to challenging or traumatic experiences, children often develop coping mechanisms to protect themselves from emotional pain. These coping mechanisms may include avoidance, emotional suppression, or maladaptive behaviors. While these coping strategies may have served a protective function in childhood, they can become entrenched patterns that persist into adulthood, hindering emotional growth and intimacy.

Formation of attachment styles

Early attachment experiences with caregivers are crucial in shaping our attachment styles and interpersonal relationships later in life. Secure attachment, characterized by trust and emotional availability, fosters healthy relationships and a sense of security. Insecure attachment, conversely, can manifest as anxious, avoidant, or disorganized attachment styles, leading to difficulties in forming and maintaining intimate connections.

Impact on emotional regulation

Childhood experiences influence our ability to regulate emotions and cope with stress. Children who grow up in nurturing and supportive environments learn healthy emotional regulation skills, such as identifying and expressing emotions effectively. In contrast, children who experience neglect, abuse, or trauma may struggle with dysregulated emotions, leading to difficulties in managing stress, anxiety, or anger in adulthood.

Influence on self-concept and identity

Our childhood experiences shape our sense of self and identity. Positive experiences that affirm our worth and value contribute to a healthy self-concept and a strong sense of identity. Conversely, negative experiences, such as criticism or rejection, can erode self-esteem and lead to shame or inadequacy. These early experiences form the foundation of our self-concept, influencing how we perceive ourselves and interact with the world around us.

Our childhood experiences leave a lasting imprint on our inner child, shaping our beliefs, behaviors, and emotional responses throughout our lives. By understanding the impact of these experiences, we can begin to unravel the layers of our inner child and embark on a journey of healing and self-discovery.

2.3 Recognizing the inner child's voice

As we embark on the journey of healing and self-discovery, it's essential to learn to recognize the voice of our inner child. This voice often speaks to us through emotions, memories, and behavior patterns rooted in our childhood experiences. By tuning into this voice, we can gain valuable insights into our deepest wounds and unmet needs, paving the way for healing and transformation.

2.3.1 Understanding emotional triggers

Emotional triggers are potent signals that alert us to the presence of our inner child. These triggers often stem from past experiences that left a profound emotional imprint, such as trauma, neglect, or abandonment. When we encounter situations or interactions resembling past experiences, our inner child may react instinctively, triggering intense emotional responses.

For example, a simple disagreement with a loved one may evoke fear, anger, or sadness that seems disproportionate to the situation. These emotional reactions may be indicative of unresolved childhood wounds triggered by present-day events. By paying attention to these emotional triggers, we can unravel the underlying causes and address the deeper needs of our inner child.

2.3.2 Identifying patterns of behavior

Patterns of behavior offer valuable clues to the presence of our inner child. These patterns often manifest as repetitive thoughts, habits, or reactions that reflect unresolved issues from our past. For example, repeatedly seeking validation or approval from others may indicate a more profound longing for acceptance and love that originated in childhood.

Similarly, if we struggle with setting boundaries or asserting our needs, it may stem from a fear of rejection or abandonment ingrained in us during childhood. By examining these behavior patterns with compassion and curiosity, we can uncover the underlying wounds and beliefs driving them.

Recognizing the voice of our inner child requires patience, self-awareness, and a willingness to explore our emotional landscape with honesty and compassion. As we learn to listen to this voice with empathy and understanding, we can begin to nurture and heal our inner child, fostering a sense of wholeness and integration within ourselves.

2.4 Healing strategies for the inner child

Healing the inner child involves a journey of self-discovery, compassion, and transformation. We can create a nurturing environment for our inner child to heal and thrive by employing various strategies and practices. Here are some effective healing strategies to consider:

1) Inner child meditation

Regular meditation practices can help us connect with our inner child more deeply. Through guided imagery and visualization, we can create a safe and loving space within ourselves where our inner child feels seen, heard, and valued. By offering affirmations and words of comfort, we can cultivate a sense of trust and security within our inner child, paving the way for healing and integration.

2) Journaling exercises

Journaling can be a powerful tool for exploring our inner world and processing our emotions. By setting aside time each day to write about our thoughts, feelings, and experiences, we can gain insight into the inner workings of our minds and hearts. Writing letters to our inner child, expressing gratitude, and practicing self-compassion can help us nurture our inner child and foster a sense of wholeness and healing.

3) Inner child dialogue

Engaging in inner child dialogue involves having conversations with our inner child to uncover and address unresolved issues from the past. By tuning into the voice of our inner child and listening with empathy and compassion, we can validate their feelings and experiences, offering comfort and support where need. Through this process of inner dialogue, we can begin to heal old wounds and cultivate a more profound sense of self-awareness and acceptance.

4) Creative expression

Expressive arts such as painting, drawing, writing, and dancing can provide influential outlets for healing and self-expression. By engaging in creative activities that resonate with our inner child, we can tap into our innate creativity and imagination, allowing our inner child to express themselves freely and authentically. Through journaling, storytelling, or artistic creation, creative expression can help us reconnect with our inner child and access deeper layers of healing and transformation.

5) Inner child workshops and retreats

Participating in workshops and retreats focused on inner child healing can provide valuable opportunities for growth and self-discovery. These immersive experiences often incorporate guided exercises, group discussions, and therapeutic techniques to support inner child healing and integration. By connecting with like-minded individuals and receiving guidance from experienced facilitators, we can gain new insights and perspectives on our healing journey.

6) Therapeutic modalities

Seeking support from a qualified therapist or counselor trained in inner child work can offer personalized guidance and support on our healing journey. Therapeutic modalities such as inner child therapy, EMDR, and somatic experiencing can help us explore and process traumatic memories, release emotional blockages, and cultivate greater self-awareness and resilience. Through the therapeutic relationship, we can receive the compassionate support and guidance needed to heal our inner child and embrace our most authentic selves.

Incorporating these healing strategies into our daily lives can create a supportive and nurturing environment for our inner child to heal and flourish. Through patience, self-compassion, and commitment to our healing journey, we can reclaim our wholeness and embrace our fullness.

2.5 Integration and transformation

Integration and transformation are critical aspects of the inner child's healing process, leading to greater wholeness and self-awareness. As we journey through healing our inner child, we gradually integrate fragmented aspects of ourselves and reclaim lost parts of our identity. Here are some important considerations for achieving integration and transformation:

Acceptance and forgiveness

Central to the integration process is the practice of acceptance and forgiveness. By acknowledging and accepting all aspects of ourselves, including our flaws, weaknesses, and past mistakes, we create space for healing and growth. Forgiving ourselves and others for past hurts and transgressions allows us to release the emotional baggage we've been carrying and move forward with greater clarity and compassion.

Emotional regulation

Learning to regulate our emotions is essential for achieving integration and transformation. By developing healthy coping mechanisms and self-soothing techniques, we can effectively manage stress, anxiety, and other challenging emotions that may arise during the healing process. We can cultivate inner peace and emotional resilience through mindfulness practices such as deep breathing, meditation, and progressive muscle relaxation.

Inner child empowerment

Empowering our inner child involves recognizing their inherent worth and value and giving them a voice. By honoring their needs, desires, and emotions, we can create a sense of safety and security within ourselves. Empowering our inner child allows us to embrace our authentic selves and live authentically and purposefully.

Boundary setting

Establishing healthy boundaries is crucial for maintaining our emotional and psychological well-being. By clearly defining and communicating our boundaries assertively, we protect ourselves from harmful influences and honor our needs and values. Setting boundaries with others also helps us cultivate healthier relationships built on mutual respect and trust.

Self-compassion and self-care

Practicing self-compassion and self-care is vital for nurturing ourselves and promoting inner healing. We create an atmosphere of love and acceptance by treating ourselves with kindness, understanding, and compassion. Engaging in self-care activities such as exercise, healthy eating, adequate rest, and relaxation helps us replenish our energy and maintain balance.

Lifestyle changes

Making positive lifestyle changes can support our inner child healing journey and improve our well-being. This may involve adopting healthier habits such as regular exercise, balanced nutrition, adequate sleep, and stress management techniques. By prioritizing our physical, mental, and emotional health, we create a solid foundation for inner transformation and growth.

Spiritual connection

Cultivating a deeper spiritual connection can provide profound support and guidance on our healing journey. Through prayer, meditation, or spiritual practices, connecting with a higher power can offer comfort, strength, and clarity during challenging times. Nurturing our spiritual well-being allows us to tap into a source of infinite love and wisdom, guiding us toward greater wholeness and fulfillment.

Integration and transformation are ongoing processes that require patience, commitment, and self-reflection. By embracing these principles and incorporating them into our daily lives, we can experience profound healing and personal growth, leading to a renewed sense of purpose and fulfillment.

Chapter 3: Catholic foundations for healing

3.1 Sacramental grace and healing

In the Catholic tradition, the sacraments are regarded as tangible expressions of God's grace, offering profound avenues for healing and spiritual renewal. Here's how the sacraments contribute to the healing process:

3.1.1 Reconciliation: embracing forgiveness and healing

The sacrament of reconciliation, also known as confession, provides a powerful means for individuals to confront their faults, seek forgiveness, and experience spiritual healing. By acknowledging our shortcomings and seeking reconciliation with God and others, we open ourselves to the transformative power of divine mercy.

Through heartfelt confession and genuine repentance, individuals can unburden themselves of guilt and shame, experiencing the liberating embrace of God's forgiveness.

3.1.2 Eucharist: nourishment for body and soul

Central to the Catholic faith, the Eucharist holds profound significance as the source and summit of Christian life. Through the Eucharist's reception, believers encounter Christ's real presence, receiving spiritual nourishment and sustenance for their journey of healing and transformation. The Eucharist serves as a sacred banquet where individuals commune with God and fellow believers, finding solace, strength, and renewal in the body and blood of Christ.

3.1.3 Anointing of the sick: healing and comfort in times of affliction

The sacrament of the anointing of the sick offers comfort, strength, and spiritual healing to those facing illness or suffering. Administered by a priest, this sacrament invokes the grace of the Holy Spirit to bring physical, emotional, and spiritual healing to the recipient. Through the anointing with blessed oil and the prayers of the faith community, individuals are invited to entrust themselves to God's loving care, finding peace and consolation amidst their afflictions.

3.2 Prayer and intercession

Prayer is a foundational aspect of Catholic spirituality. It offers a direct line of communication with God and serves as a powerful tool for healing and transformation. Prayer takes on various forms within healing, each playing a vital role in fostering spiritual well-being and inner peace.

Personal prayer forms the cornerstone of the Christian life, providing individuals with a sacred space to commune with God in intimacy and sincerity. Through personal prayer, individuals can express their deepest desires, fears, and hopes to God, knowing they are heard and cherished. Whether through structured prayers like the Our Father or spontaneous conversations with the Divine, personal prayer cultivates a sense of connection and trust in God's providence, offering solace and strength in times of need.

Intercessory prayer entails lifting the needs and concerns of others to God, acting as a channel of God's grace and compassion for those suffering. As members of the Body of Christ, believers are called to intercede on behalf of their brothers and sisters, standing in solidarity with them in their joys and sorrows.

Intercessory prayer not only invokes God's healing touch upon the lives of others but also fosters a sense of communal support and empathy within the faith community. By entrusting the needs of others into God's loving hands, intercessors participate in God's redemptive work in the world, offering hope and consolation to those in distress.

Liturgical prayer encompasses the communal worship and praise of the faith community, uniting believers in a shared expression of faith and devotion. Through liturgical prayers, such as the Mass, the Liturgy of the Hours, and devotional practices, Catholics participate in the Church's sacramental life, drawing strength and inspiration from the rich tradition of Christian worship.

Within the context of healing, liturgical prayer serves as a source of consolation, renewal, and transformation, inviting individuals to encounter the healing presence of Christ amid the worshipping community. As believers gather to offer their prayers and praises to God, they are united in a sacred bond of fellowship and communion, finding solace and healing in the embrace of the Body of Christ.

3.3 Spiritual direction and guidance

Spiritual direction is a time-honored tradition within the Catholic Church. It offers individuals personalized guidance and support on their spiritual journey. Rooted in the belief that God speaks to each person uniquely, spiritual direction provides a sacred space for individuals to discern God's presence and invitations in their lives, deepening their relationship with the Divine and fostering spiritual growth and transformation.

3.3.1 Understanding Spiritual Direction

At its core, spiritual direction is a collaborative process between a trained spiritual director and a director, wherein the director shares their experiences, questions, and insights. In contrast, the spiritual director listens attentively and offers Discernment and guidance. Unlike counseling or therapy, spiritual direction focuses primarily on the individual's relationship with God, exploring how God works and inviting them to respond with openness and trust. Through reflective listening, Discernment, and prayerful accompaniment, spiritual directors help navigate the complexities of the spiritual life, offering insights and resources to support their faith journey.

3.3.2 The role of the spiritual direction

Your spiritual director is not just a guide, but a compassionate companion on your spiritual journey. They draw upon their own experience and training to accompany you with compassion and wisdom. They may not have all the answers, but they offer a listening ear, a compassionate heart, and a discerning spirit. They create a safe and supportive environment for you to explore your relationship with God. By asking probing questions, offering spiritual exercises, and providing resources for prayer and reflection, they empower you to deepen your awareness of God's presence and discern God's will in your life.

3.3.3 The process of spiritual direction

Spiritual direction is not about someone telling you what to do, but about empowering you to navigate your spiritual journey. It typically involves regular meetings between you and your spiritual director, ranging from monthly to quarterly sessions, depending on your needs and preferences. During these sessions, you have the opportunity to share your joys, struggles, and questions. Your spiritual director offers attentive listening, compassionate feedback, and spiritual guidance. Through prayerful conversation, reflective listening, and discernment exercises, spiritual direction helps you cultivate a deeper awareness of God's presence and invitations in your life, fostering your spiritual growth and transformation over time.

3.3.4 Discernment and Decision-making

A key aspect of spiritual direction is discernment, which is prayerfully seeking God's will and guidance in making decisions and navigating life's challenges. Spiritual directors assist in discerning the movements of the Holy Spirit in their lives, helping them distinguish between the promptings of God and the influences of ego, fear, or societal expectations. Through prayer, reflection, and dialogue, spiritual direction is equipped with the tools and discernment skills needed to make wise and faithful decisions aligned with God's plan for their lives. By surrendering to God's guidance and trusting in divine providence, you will embark on a journey of spiritual Discernment and transformation guided by the wisdom and grace of the Holy Spirit.

3.4 Wisdom and reflection on the Scriptures

Scripture serves as a wellspring of wisdom and inspiration for Catholics seeking healing and wholeness. Through the sacred texts of the Bible, individuals encounter stories of God's love, mercy, and redemption, finding solace, guidance, and hope in times of trial and tribulation. Here, we explore the significance of scriptural wisdom and reflection in the journey of healing and transformation.

The Bible, a compilation of the Old and New Testaments, is not just a historical document, but a living guide that resonates with the human condition and the divine plan for salvation. From the creation story in Genesis to the life and teachings of Jesus Christ in the Gospels, Scripture offers timeless truths and eternal principles that are as relevant today as they were centuries ago, illuminating the path to healing and wholeness.

One of the central themes of Scripture is God's steadfast love and faithfulness towards humanity. Throughout the Old Testament, God's covenant relationship with His people is depicted through stories of liberation, forgiveness, and renewal. From the Exodus narrative to the prophets' calls for justice and mercy, Scripture reveals God's enduring commitment to healing and restoring His creation.

In the New Testament, the person of Jesus Christ emerges as the embodiment of God's love and compassion. Through His teachings, miracles, and ultimately, His sacrificial death and resurrection, Jesus offers hope and redemption to all seeking healing and reconciliation. His ministry is characterized by compassion for the sick, the marginalized, and the broken-hearted, demonstrating God's desire to heal and transform every aspect of human life.

Scripture also provides practical guidance for living a life of faith and discipleship. The Old Testament wisdom literature, including the Psalms, Proverbs, and Ecclesiastes, offers timeless insights into the human experience, addressing themes of suffering, wisdom, and virtue. These texts invite readers to reflect on their own lives and experiences, finding resonance and relevance in the timeless truths contained within.

For Catholics, the practice of Lectio Divina, or sacred reading, is not just a ritual but a personal encounter with the living Word of God. This ancient spiritual practice involves reading, meditating, praying, and contemplating the Word of God, allowing its message to penetrate the depths of one's heart and soul. Through Lectio Divina, individuals open themselves to the promptings of the Holy Spirit, allowing Scripture to speak directly to their unique circumstances and needs.

The Catholic tradition emphasizes the communal dimension of Scripture, encouraging believers to encounter the Word of God within the context of the faith community. Catholics engage with Scripture as a living and dynamic source of grace and inspiration through liturgical celebrations, communal prayer, and shared reflection on the Sunday readings.

Scripture is a collection of words and a gateway to encounter the living God and experience His transformative power in our lives. Through prayerful reflection on the Word of God, we are not just reading but entering into a deeper relationship with Christ, the divine physician who offers healing, wholeness, and abundant life to all who seek Him. As we immerse ourselves in the sacred texts of Scripture, we discover anew the profound truth that God's Word is a lamp unto our feet and a light unto our path, guiding us on the journey of healing and transformation.

3.5 Support and fellowship in the community

In the Catholic tradition, community support and fellowship play vital roles in the journey of healing and spiritual growth. Through shared prayer, mutual encouragement, and compassionate companionship, individuals find strength, solace, and solidarity as they navigate life's challenges and seek wholeness in Christ. Here, we explore the significance of community support and fellowship in fostering healing and renewal within the Catholic faith.

3.5.1 The power of community

At the heart of Catholic spirituality lies the belief in the communion of saints, the mystical union of all believers across time and space. This communion extends beyond earthly boundaries, encompassing both the Church's living and departed members. Within this spiritual community, individuals find support, mediation, and solidarity in their journey towards healing and holiness.

One primary way Catholics experience community support is through participation in the Church's life. Celebrating the sacraments, particularly the Eucharist, serves as a source of nourishment and strength for believers, uniting them in a common bond of faith and love. Through the Church's sacramental life, individuals encounter Christ's presence in their midst, receiving His grace and mercy for the journey ahead.

Catholic communities, with their diverse parish groups, prayer circles, and faith-sharing communities, offer a welcoming space for individuals to connect with others who share their beliefs and values. These communities, built on a foundation of mutual trust, respect, and compassion, provide a profound sense of belonging and acceptance, making each individual feel valued and integral to the community.

3.5.2 Journeying Together in Christ

Central to the Catholic understanding of community is journeying together in Christ. Just as Jesus walked alongside His disciples on the road to Emmaus, so are Catholics called to accompany one another on the faith journey. This spirit of accompaniment involves listening, empathizing, and supporting one another in times of joy and sorrow, triumph and trial.

Within Catholic communities, individuals find companionship and solidarity in their shared experiences of healing and transformation.

Whether through prayer meetings, support groups, or pastoral counseling, Catholics come together to offer not just comfort and encouragement, but also a beacon of hope and a source of resilience in times of crisis or adversity. The strength of the community becomes a reassuring presence, instilling hope and resilience in individuals facing life's challenges.

Moreover, the Catholic tradition emphasizes the importance of bearing burdens and sharing in each other's joys. Through acts of charity, mercy, and kindness, Catholics demonstrate their commitment to the common good and the welfare of all community members. By extending a helping hand to those in need, individuals embody the love of Christ and fulfill the Gospel mandate to love one another as He has loved us.

Community support and fellowship are essential aspects of the Catholic faith, providing a nurturing environment for healing, growth, and renewal. By participating actively in the life of the Church and journeying together in Christ, individuals discover the transformative power of community as they seek to become more fully alive in the love of God. Through mutual care and solidarity, Catholics bear witness to the reality that we are all members of one body, called to share in each other's joys and sorrows, triumphs and struggles, as we walk together on the path of discipleship.

Chapter 4: The role of self-help in Catholicism

4.1 Historical context of self-help in Catholicism

The concept of self-help in Catholicism has deep historical roots, reflecting the Church's longstanding focus on personal growth and spiritual development. From its earliest days, the Church has encouraged believers to strive for holiness and self-improvement, emphasizing the importance of inner transformation as a path to spiritual fulfillment.

In the early Christian era, the Church Fathers, such as St. Augustine and St. Jerome, wrote extensively about the need for personal reflection and self-discipline. These early theologians believed that self-examination and repentance were crucial for spiritual growth. St. Augustine, for example, in his "Confessions," emphasized the importance of introspection and self-awareness in understanding one's relationship with God. His works highlight that knowing oneself is vital in drawing closer to the divine.

During the medieval period, self-help continued to evolve within Catholicism. Monasticism played a significant role in promoting personal discipline and self-improvement. Monks and nuns adhered to strict rules of conduct and regularly practiced prayer, fasting, and manual labor. The Rule of St. Benedict, written in the 6th century, is a prime example. It provided a structured approach to monastic life, emphasizing the importance of balance between prayer, work, and study, encouraging a holistic approach to personal and spiritual development.

The Renaissance and Reformation periods brought further developments in the Catholic approach to self-help. During the Counter-Reformation, the Catholic Church responded to the challenges posed by Protestant reformers by emphasizing personal piety and spiritual renewal. This era saw the rise of influential figures such as St. Ignatius of Loyola, founder of the Jesuit order, who developed the "Spiritual Exercises." This compilation of prayers, meditations, and contemplative practices aimed to help individuals deepen their spiritual lives and foster a closer relationship with God through self-reflection and disciplined effort. Their contributions continue to inspire and shape the concept of self-help in Catholicism.

In the modern era, the Catholic Church continues to support self-help, though it is often framed within the broader context of spiritual growth and community support. The Second Vatican Council (1962-1965) brought significant changes to the Church, encouraging a more active engagement of laypeople in their faith and promoting personal responsibility for one's spiritual journey. This shift has led to various programs and movements within the Church that emphasize personal development, such as retreats, spiritual direction, and faith-based counseling.

The historical context of self-help in Catholicism reveals a rich tradition of encouraging personal growth and spiritual development. From the writings of the early Church Fathers and the structured life of monasticism to the spiritual exercises of St. Ignatius and the modern emphasis on lay participation, the Catholic Church has long recognized the importance of self-improvement as a means of achieving spiritual fulfillment and a closer relationship with God. This emphasis on personal journey underscores the individual's empowerment and responsibility in their spiritual growth.

4.2 The theological foundations of self-help

The concept of self-help within Catholicism is deeply rooted in its theological foundations. These foundations provide a framework for understanding how personal growth and spiritual development align with the teachings of the Church. By exploring key theological principles, we can better appreciate the role of self-help in the Catholic faith.

4.2.1 Human Dignity and the Image of God

At the heart of Catholic theology is the belief in the inherent dignity of every human being. This belief is grounded in the doctrine of Imago Dei, which asserts that humans are created in the image and likeness of God (Genesis 1:26-27). This understanding emphasizes that every person has intrinsic worth and potential. Consequently, self-help is seen as a means to recognize and cultivate this God-given dignity. By striving for personal growth, individuals honor the divine image within themselves, aligning their lives more closely with God's will.

4.2.2 The call to holiness

The Catholic Church teaches that all people are called to holiness. This universal call, articulated in documents like Lumen Gentium from the Second Vatican Council, underscores that every person is invited to pursue a life of virtue and sanctity. Self-help practices, such as self-examination, prayer, and acts of charity, are tools that help individuals respond to this call. By engaging in these practices, Catholics work towards personal transformation, seeking to embody the virtues exemplified by Christ and the saints.

4.2.3 Grace and cooperation with God

Catholic theology emphasizes the importance of Grace—God's free and unmerited favor—for salvation and personal growth. However, it also teaches that humans must cooperate with this Grace through their actions. This cooperation is known as synergy, where human effort and divine Grace work together in sanctification. From a Catholic perspective, self-help involves actively participating in this cooperative relationship with God. Practices such as regular prayer, participation in the sacraments, and spiritual disciplines allow individuals to open themselves to God's Grace and work toward their spiritual growth.

4.2.4 Community and the Body of Christ

The Catholic understanding of self-help is not a solitary journey, but a deeply communal one. The Church is viewed as the Body of Christ, with each member playing a vital role in the health and growth of the whole community. This communal aspect is not just a nice addition, but a crucial part of self-help in Catholicism. It highlights that personal development and spiritual growth are not just individual pursuits, but are supported and enriched by the community. Engaging in self-help within the Catholic context often involves participating in communal activities such as attending Mass, joining prayer groups, and seeking guidance from spiritual directors. These communal practices provide support, accountability, and encouragement, helping individuals grow in their faith and personal lives.

The theological foundations of self-help in Catholicism encompass a profound respect for human dignity, a universal call to holiness, the necessity of cooperating with divine Grace, and the importance of Community. By understanding these principles, we can see how self-help practices are compatible with Catholic teachings and integral to living out one's faith. These practices help individuals to grow in virtue, deepen their relationship with God, and contribute to the well-being of the Church community, ultimately leading to a more fulfilling and spiritually enriched life.

4.3 Integrate faith and personal development

Integrating faith and personal development is a holistic approach that acknowledges the interconnectedness of spiritual and personal growth. This integration is essential for leading a fulfilling and meaningful life in the Catholic tradition. It involves aligning one's personal development goals with the teachings and values of the Catholic faith, ensuring that efforts towards self-improvement are grounded in spiritual principles.

At the core of this integration is the belief that personal growth is not just about achieving success or self-fulfillment in a worldly sense but about becoming the person God intends each individual to be. This perspective shifts the focus from purely secular self-help practices to those that nurture the soul and the mind. For Catholics, personal development activities, such as setting goals, developing positive habits, and seeking emotional healing, are approached with a spiritual dimension.

Regular prayer and reflection are practical ways to integrate faith and personal development. Prayer provides a foundation for personal growth by fostering a deeper relationship with God, offering guidance, and helping to discern God's will. Reflection, mainly through spiritual practices like the Examen, encourages individuals to review their daily actions, recognize areas for growth, and seek God's grace to improve. This daily practice ensures that personal development remains aligned with faith values.

The sacraments play a crucial role in this integration. Participation in the sacraments, especially the Eucharist and Reconciliation, offers spiritual nourishment and renewal. The Eucharist strengthens the bond with Christ and the Church community, providing spiritual sustenance for the journey of personal growth. Conversely, reconciliation offers a path to healing and forgiveness, essential components of personal development. By regularly partaking in these sacraments, Catholics receive the grace needed to pursue personal transformation in a spiritually enriching way.

Community support is another vital aspect of integrating faith and personal development. The Catholic Church provides a support network through various ministries, groups, and spiritual mentors. Engaging with this community offers encouragement, accountability, and wisdom from others who share the same faith and values. Whether through Bible study groups, support groups, or spiritual direction, the community helps individuals stay on track and grow personally and spiritually.

Finally, living out the virtues is a key element of this integration. Humility, patience, charity, and temperance guide personal development efforts. Striving to cultivate these virtues ensures that pursuing personal goals does not become self-centered but remains oriented toward serving God and others. This virtuous living is a practical expression of integrating faith into daily actions and personal growth.

Integrating faith and personal development in the Catholic tradition involves prayer and reflection, participation in the sacraments, community support, and cultivating virtues. This holistic approach ensures that personal growth is not only about achieving worldly success but also about growing closer to God and fulfilling one's spiritual potential.

4.4 The role of prayer in self-help

Prayer plays a pivotal role in self-help, especially within the context of Catholicism. It bridges personal development and spiritual growth, offering a profound way to connect with God, seek guidance, and find inner peace. Understanding the multifaceted role of prayer in self-help can enhance one's journey toward personal transformation.

First and foremost, prayer provides clarity and direction. Prayer can be a source of divine guidance in moments of confusion or uncertainty. When setting personal goals or making significant life decisions, prayer can help individuals discern the right path. This connection to a higher power ensures that decisions are aligned with spiritual values and God's will.

Another pivotal role of prayer in self-help is its power to nurture gratitude and a positive outlook. Gratitude prayers serve as a reminder to acknowledge and value the blessings in one's life, shifting the focus from what is lacking to what is abundant. This optimistic perspective can have a profound impact on mental and emotional well-being, fostering a more positive and resilient attitude.

Prayer also plays a critical role in self-reflection and personal accountability. Examining one's actions, thoughts, and intentions through prayer can lead to greater self-awareness. This self-awareness is crucial for personal growth, as it allows individuals to identify areas for improvement and seek God's help in making necessary changes. Regularly confessing and seeking forgiveness through prayer reinforces the commitment to personal growth and ethical living.

Prayer provides emotional healing and comfort. Prayer can offer solace and healing in times of pain, sorrow, or emotional turmoil. By sharing burdens with God, individuals can experience relief from emotional distress and gain the strength to move forward. Prayer offers a safe space to express emotions and seek comfort, facilitating emotional healing. Through prayer, individuals can find divine support, a source of strength during difficult times.

Prayer fosters a sense of community and connectedness. Praying with others builds a supportive community, whether in a church setting, prayer group, or family. This sense of belonging and shared faith can enhance one's self-help journey, providing encouragement and accountability. Group prayers strengthen community bonds and provide mutual support in personal growth efforts. Praying with others reinforces a collective commitment to spiritual and personal development.

Prayer is a vital component of self-help in the Catholic tradition. It provides guidance, cultivates gratitude, encourages self-reflection, offers emotional healing, and fosters community. By integrating prayer into their daily lives, individuals can align their development efforts with their spiritual journey, ensuring a holistic approach to growth and transformation.

4.5 Catholic Saints and self-improvement

Catholic saints have long been role models for self-improvement and personal growth. Their lives offer a wealth of wisdom and practical advice for those seeking to better themselves. By looking at their journeys, we can find inspiration and guidance in our quests for self-improvement. Here are four key aspects where saints can help us in this journey.

1) Perseverance in adversity

Many saints faced significant challenges and hardships but persevered with unwavering faith. For instance, Saint Teresa of Ávila encountered numerous difficulties reforming the Carmelite order. Despite opposition and illness, she remained steadfast in her mission. Her story teaches us the importance of perseverance. We will likely face obstacles when pursuing self-improvement, but the saints' example reminds us to stay committed and trust in God's plan.

2) Humility and self-awareness

Humility is a cornerstone of many saints' lives. Saint Francis of Assisi is a prime example. He renounced his wealth and lived a life of poverty and humility. His story teaches us about the value of self-awareness and humility in self-improvement. Recognizing our flaws and seeking to improve them is crucial for personal growth. Saint Francis's life encourages us to look inward, acknowledge our shortcomings, and strive to become better versions of ourselves.

3) Devotion to prayer

Prayer was central to the lives of many saints, and it played a crucial role in their personal development. Saint Thérèse of Lisieux, known as the Little Flower, emphasized the power of prayer in her "little way" of seeking holiness through small, everyday actions. Her approach shows that regular prayer can help us stay grounded and focused on our goals. By incorporating prayer into our daily routines, we can seek divine guidance and strength in our self-improvement efforts.

4) Service to others

Many saints dedicated their lives to serving others, which in turn helped them grow personally and spiritually. Saint Mother Teresa of Calcutta is a shining example. Her selfless service to the poorest of the poor demonstrated profound love and compassion. Her life reminds us that helping others can be a powerful catalyst for self-improvement. By focusing on the needs of others, we can develop empathy, patience, and kindness—qualities essential for personal growth.

Catholic saints provide a rich source of inspiration and practical advice for those seeking self-improvement. Their lives illustrate the importance of perseverance, humility, prayer, and service to others. Following their examples, we can navigate our paths to personal growth with faith and determination. The saints show us that self-improvement is not just about achieving personal success but also about growing closer to God and serving those around us.

4.6 Modern catholic perspectives on self-help

In the realm of self-help and personal development, Catholics offer a unique perspective. Modern Catholic thinkers and leaders not only acknowledge the significance of self-help but also stress its alignment with faith and spiritual growth. Let's delve into how contemporary Catholic views seamlessly blend self-help principles with the faith.

For modern Catholics, self-improvement is not just about personal goals, but also about drawing closer to God. This holistic approach to self-help means that while setting goals and working on personal development, one should always prioritize spiritual growth. For Catholics, self-help encompasses the mind, body, and soul.

Modern Catholic perspectives often highlight the importance of integrating faith into daily self-improvement practices. For example:

- *prayer and reflection*: regular prayer and reflection are seen as essential. They provide the spiritual foundation for personal growth. Catholics are encouraged to take time each day to pray, meditate, and reflect on their lives, seeking God's guidance in their self-improvement journey;

- *community support*: engaging with the community is also crucial. Being part of a faith community provides support, encouragement, and accountability. It's about growing together and helping each other on the path of self-improvement;

- *sacraments*: participation in the sacraments, especially the Eucharist and Confession, is considered vital. These sacraments are seen as sources of grace and strength, helping individuals to overcome their weaknesses and grow in virtue.

Modern Catholic thinkers also emphasize the importance of balancing personal ambition with humility and service to others. Self-improvement should never become self-centered. Instead, it should lead to greater love and service. This aligns with the teachings of many saints who saw personal growth as a means to better serve God and others.

Another critical point is the integration of modern psychological insights with traditional Catholic teachings. Many Catholics today look to incorporate insights from psychology and therapy into their self-help practices, ensuring these insights do not contradict their faith.

Practices like mindfulness and seeking therapy for mental health issues are encouraged as long as they are consistent with Catholic values.

Emphasizing personal responsibility and the importance of making morally good choices is central. Self-help should empower individuals to live virtuous lives according to the teachings of the Church.

Modern Catholic perspectives on self-help integrate personal development with spiritual growth. They emphasize prayer, community support, the sacraments, and balancing personal ambition with humility and service. By following these principles, Catholics can pursue self-improvement that enriches their faith and brings them closer to God.

Chapter 5: Cultivating inner joy

5.1 Rediscovering the wonder of childhood

Remember how everything seemed magical as kids? From chasing butterflies to building forts out of blankets, we were masters at finding wonder in the smallest things. But as adults, that sense of awe often gets lost in the shuffle of responsibilities and routines. So, how can we bring back that childlike wonder into our lives?

One way is to reconnect with nature. Stroll in the park, watch the sunset, or sit under a tree and listen to the birds chirping. Nature has a way of sparking wonder and reminding us of the beauty in the world around us.

So, kick off your shoes, and feel the grass beneath your feet – it's like hitting the reset button for your soul.

Another way to rediscover childhood wonder is through creativity. Remember how you used to doodle on everything from napkins to textbooks? Well, it's time to dust off those artistic skills and let your imagination run wild. Whether painting, writing, or just doodling, creative expression can reignite that spark of wonder and curiosity within you.

And let's not forget about the power of exploration. As kids, we were always eager to explore new places and try new things. So why not channel that adventurous spirit and embark on your own mini-adventure? It could be as simple as pushing a new restaurant or taking a spontaneous road trip. The key is stepping outside your comfort zone and embracing the unknown.

Don't underestimate the joy of simple pleasures. Whether it's blowing bubbles, flying a kite, or playing with a pet, sometimes the little things bring us the most joy. So, don't be afraid to let your inner child come out to play – after all, life is too short to take too seriously.

By tapping into these simple yet powerful practices, you can rediscover that sense of wonder and excitement that made childhood so magical. So go ahead, embrace your inner child, and let the wonder of the world wash over you.

5.2 Cultivating creative expression

Ever notice how, as kids, we were always doodling, crafting, and dreaming up imaginative worlds? Creative expression was second nature to us back then, but as adults, we often push aside our artistic impulses in favor of more practical pursuits. However, nurturing our creativity is essential for maintaining a sense of joy and fulfillment in life. Here's how you can cultivate creative expression in your everyday life:

Make time for play

Remember when playtime was the highlight of your day? Whether building LEGO towers or staging epic battles with action figures, play was integral to childhood. As adults, we may not have as much time for play, but that doesn't mean we can't incorporate elements of it into our lives. Set aside time each week to engage in activities that bring you joy and allow your imagination to run wild. Whether painting, drawing, or playing a musical instrument, permitting yourself to play can reignite your creative spark.

Embrace imperfection

One of the most significant barriers to creativity is the fear of failure. As kids, we weren't afraid to make mistakes – in fact, we often embraced them as opportunities to learn and grow. Somewhere along the way, many of us lose that fearlessness and become overly critical of our creative endeavors. But the truth is that creativity thrives in an environment where mistakes are welcome. So, permit yourself to create imperfectly. Allow yourself to experiment, take risks, and make mistakes. Remember, it's not about creating a masterpiece – it's about the process of self-expression and exploration.

Find inspiration in everyday life

Creativity is all around us – we just have to open our eyes to see it. Take time to notice the beauty in the world around you, whether it's the vibrant colors of a sunset or the intricate patterns of a spider's web. Please pay attention to the small details that often go unnoticed and allow them to inspire your creative pursuits. Keep a journal or sketchbook handy to capture your observations and ideas. You never know where inspiration might strike!

Experiment with different mediums

Creativity knows no bounds, so don't hesitate to step outside your comfort zone and try new things. Experiment with different artistic mediums – from painting and drawing to sculpting and photography. Each medium offers unique challenges and possibilities, allowing you to explore various aspects of your creativity. You might discover a hidden talent or passion along the way!

Share your creations with others

Creativity is meant to be shared, so don't keep your creations to yourself. Share your artwork, writing, music, or whatever form your creative expression takes with friends, family, or strangers online. Not only does sharing your work provide validation and encouragement, but it also allows you to connect with others who share your interests and passions. Plus, seeing your creations through someone else's eyes can offer new insights and perspectives that enrich your creative journey.

By making time for play, embracing imperfection, finding inspiration in everyday life, experimenting with different mediums, and sharing your creations with others, you can cultivate a thriving creative practice that brings joy, fulfillment, and self-expression into your life. So unleash your inner artist, and let your creativity soar!

5.3 Embracing playfulness in everyday life

Remember the carefree days of childhood when playing was our primary occupation? As adults, we often lose touch with that sense of playfulness amidst the responsibilities and stresses of daily life. However, embracing playfulness can bring joy, spontaneity, and creativity into our lives, fostering a more lighthearted and fulfilling existence. This shift in mindset can lead to a more positive outlook, increased resilience, and a deeper sense of well-being.

5.3.1 Rediscovering the joy of play

Think back to your favorite childhood games and activities – perhaps building forts out of blankets, playing tag with friends, or pretending to be superheroes saving the world. These playful pursuits weren't just a way to pass the time but a source of pure joy and excitement. As adults, we may dismiss play as frivolous or childish. Still, the truth is that incorporating play into our lives can have profound benefits for our mental, emotional, and physical well-being.

One way to rediscover the joy of play is to reconnect with activities that bring you pure, unadulterated delight. Whether it's swinging on a playground swing, flying a kite, or splashing in puddles on a rainy day, allow yourself to engage in activities that make you feel like a kid again. These activities, often associated with our childhood, can reignite a sense of wonder and inspire us to approach life with a more playful attitude. Remember, play isn't just for children – it's a fundamental human need that nourishes our spirits and rejuvenates our souls.

5.3.2 Cultivating a playful mindset

Embracing playfulness isn't just about engaging in specific activities; it's also about cultivating a playful mindset that permeates every aspect of our lives. A playful mindset involves approaching life with curiosity, openness, and a willingness to experiment and take risks. It's about embracing the unexpected, finding joy in the mundane, and infusing even the most routine tasks with fun and adventure.

One way to cultivate a playful mindset is to adopt a "childlike curiosity" about the world around you. Instead of rushing through life on autopilot, take time to notice the little things—the shapes of clouds in the sky, the sound of birds chirping in the morning, the way sunlight dances on the leaves of trees. This practice of being fully present in the moment allows you to approach each experience with wonder and awe, a key aspect of a playful mindset.

Another key aspect of cultivating a playful mindset is learning to laugh at yourself and not take life too seriously. Life is full of ups and downs, triumphs and setbacks, but maintaining a sense of humor can help us navigate the challenges with grace and resilience. So don't be afraid to embrace your inner goofball, indulge in silliness, and let laughter be your constant companion on life's journey.

Embracing playfulness in everyday life is essential for maintaining a sense of joy, spontaneity, and creativity. By reconnecting with the joy of play and cultivating a playful mindset, we can infuse our lives with a lightheartedness and wonder that enriches our overall well-being. So embrace your inner child, and let the spirit of playfulness guide you on your journey to a more fulfilling and joyful life.

5.4 Finding healing through inner joy

Amidst life's challenges and struggles, it's easy to lose sight of the importance of joy. Yet, embracing inner joy can be a powerful source of healing, rejuvenation, and transformation. This section'll explore how cultivating a sense of inner pleasure can contribute to our overall well-being and help us navigate life's ups and downs with grace and resilience.

5.4.1 The healing power of joy

Joy isn't just a fleeting emotion; it's a state of being that transcends circumstances and empowers us to find meaning and purpose amid adversity. When we cultivate inner joy, we create a reservoir of strength and resilience that sustains us through life's darkest moments. Joy profoundly impacts our physical, emotional, and spiritual health, promoting relaxation, reducing stress, and boosting our immune system.

One of the most remarkable aspects of joy is its contagious nature. When we experience joy, we radiate positive energy that uplifts those around us, creating a ripple effect of healing and transformation. In times of suffering and sorrow, joy serves as a beacon of hope, reminding us that even amid pain, there is still beauty, love, and light to be found.

5.4.2 Cultivating inner joy

Cultivating inner joy is not about denying or ignoring life's challenges; it's about focusing on what brings us happiness, fulfillment, and peace. It's about finding joy in life's simple pleasures – a warm cup of tea on a cold winter's day, a heartfelt conversation with a loved one, or a breathtaking sunset painting the sky with vibrant hues.

One powerful way to cultivate inner joy is through the practice of gratitude. By consciously acknowledging and appreciating the blessings in our lives, we shift our focus from scarcity to abundance, from despair to hope. Gratitude opens our hearts to the beauty and wonder of the world around us, allowing us to find joy in even the most ordinary moments.

Another key aspect of cultivating inner joy is learning to let go of expectations and embrace the present moment with an open heart and mind. Often, we sabotage our happiness by clinging to rigid expectations or dwelling on past regrets. By releasing the need for control and surrendering to the flow of life, we create space for joy to enter our lives and transform our outlook.

5.4.3 The role of inner joy in healing

Inner joy plays a crucial role in healing, providing comfort, solace, and peace amidst life's storms. When we cultivate joy, we create a sanctuary within ourselves to find refuge from the chaos and turmoil of the outside world. This inner sanctuary becomes a source of strength and resilience, empowering us to face life's challenges with courage and grace.

Moreover, inner joy profoundly impacts our relationships, fostering deeper connections and creating a sense of belonging and community. When we approach life with joy and positivity, we attract like-minded souls who share our vision for a brighter, more compassionate world. Together, we form a network of support and encouragement that sustains us through life's trials and triumphs.

Finally, seeking healing via inner pleasure entails creating a profound sense of calm, satisfaction, and contentment that permeates all aspects of our lives rather than having fleeting moments of bliss. By accepting joy as a way of life, we may turn our anguish into purpose, our sadness into strength, and our scars into insight. Allow your inner pleasure to shine brightly, blazing the way to healing and health for yourself and others.

5.5 Sharing joy with others

Sharing joy with others is a beautiful gift we give and a profound act of self-care and healing. When we spread joy, we create a ripple effect of positivity that uplifts those around us and ourselves. This section'll explore the importance of sharing joy with others and how it can enhance our well-being and deepen our connections.

Joy is contagious, and when we share it with others, we amplify its power to brighten the world. Whether through a kind word, a heartfelt smile, or a simple act of kindness, every expression of joy can touch someone's heart and inspire them to pass it on. By spreading joy, we create a chain reaction of happiness that transcends boundaries and brings people together in a spirit of love and unity.

Sarah, a busy working mom, shares her experience of how sharing joy with her family has transformed their relationships. "*I used to get so caught up in the daily grind that I forgot to pause and appreciate the little moments of joy with my family. But when I started trying to share laughter, hugs, and heartfelt conversations with them, I noticed a remarkable shift in our dynamic. We became closer, more connected, and more resilient in facing life's challenges. Now, our home is filled with love and laughter, and I'm grateful every day for the joy we share."*

John, a retiree living in a senior community, reflects on the impact of spreading joy with his fellow residents. *"As we age, it's easy to focus on our limitations and losses, but I've found that sharing joy with others can be a powerful antidote to loneliness and isolation. Whether it's organizing a game night, leading a sing-along, or simply sharing a funny story, I've seen firsthand how these small acts of kindness can brighten someone's day and create a sense of belonging and camaraderie within our community. In giving joy, we receive it tenfold, and I'm grateful for the opportunity to bring a little sunshine into the lives of my fellow residents."*

Sharing joy with others enhances our relationships and promotes our well-being and fulfillment. When we focus on lifting others and spreading positivity, we shift our attention away from our worries and insecurities, allowing us to experience a more profound sense of purpose and meaning. Moreover, acts of kindness and compassion have been shown to boost our mood, reduce stress, and improve our overall mental and emotional health.

Furthermore, sharing joy fosters a sense of connection and belonging essential for our mental and emotional well-being. When we make an effort to connect with others on a deeper level and share our joys and sorrows openly and authentically, we create a sense of community that sustains us through life's ups and downs. In a world that often feels fragmented and disconnected, sharing joy with others reminds us of our common humanity and shared journey toward love and fulfillment.

5.6 Sustaining joy with gratitude and mindfulness

It is not enough to experience brief moments of bliss to sustain joy; instead, it is necessary to cultivate an attitude of thankfulness and awareness that enables us to discover joy in the mundane moments of life. In this part of the article, we will discuss how cultivating an attitude of appreciation and mindfulness may assist us in maintaining our joy and appreciating each day's splendor.

Gratitude

Gratitude is like a superpower; it can change our vision of the world and bring greater happiness into our lives. When we create a grateful mindset, we educate our thoughts to see the gifts rather than the problems, the beauty rather than the imperfections. Recognizing and appreciating the positive aspects of our lives, no matter how minor, allows us to feel more satisfaction and contentment.

Practicing thankfulness does not have to be complicated or time-consuming. It may be as easy as taking a few minutes each day to think about what we are grateful for, whether it is the sun's warmth on our faces, the laughter of a loved one, or the beauty of nature. By intentionally changing our attention to the positive parts of our existence, we generate a chain reaction of delight that permeates every area of our being.

Mindfulness

Mindfulness is the discipline of remaining completely present in the moment, free of judgment or distraction. It is about developing a profound awareness of our thoughts, feelings, and sensations and learning to accept each moment with openness and curiosity. When we approach life with mindfulness, we become more aware of the richness of our experiences and better able to appreciate the small pleasures that delight us.

Incorporating mindfulness into our everyday lives does not have to be complicated or time-consuming. It may be as easy as taking a few deep breaths, focusing on our senses, or experiencing the feelings in our bodies as we go about our day. By returning our focus to the present moment, we release ourselves from fear and concern, allowing joy to emerge.

By practicing gratitude and mindfulness, we lay the groundwork for long-term happiness. We approach each day with an open heart and a thankful attitude, allowing joy to grow and thrive. We learn to appreciate the beauty of every moment, no matter how tiny, and to find delight in the simplest pleasures of existence.

Furthermore, gratitude and mindfulness have been found to improve our mental, emotional, and physical well-being. They can alleviate stress, boost resilience, and improve our general well-being. Making thankfulness and mindfulness a regular part of our everyday routine prepares us for a lifetime of happiness, contentment, and inner peace.

Sustaining joy entails building a thankfulness and mindfulness mentality that helps us discover delight in the present moment rather than pursuing happiness. By being grateful for our benefits and embracing each moment with awareness and presence, we lay the groundwork for long-term pleasure and satisfaction. So, let us embrace the power of thankfulness and mindfulness and let joy be our continuous companion on our journey through life.

Chapter 6: Healing practices and techniques

6.1 Physical healing mode

When it comes to healing our bodies, there are many paths we can take, and each person's journey is unique. The power to choose our healing modality is in our hands, and this choice can be a significant step towards our well-being. Physical healing modalities treat the body directly, addressing ailments and discomforts that hinder our well-being. These techniques range from traditional medical treatments to alternative therapies to restore balance and vitality.

One of the most common physical healing modalities is conventional medicine, which includes treatments like medication, surgery, and physical therapy. These approaches are often recommended by healthcare professionals and are based on scientific research and evidence. Medications help manage symptoms and alleviate pain, while surgeries can correct structural issues or remove diseased tissues. Through targeted exercises and interventions, physical therapy aims to improve mobility, strength, and function.

In addition to conventional medicine, many people explore complementary and alternative therapies to support their healing journey. These approaches emphasize holistic well-being, considering the interconnectedness of the body, mind, and spirit. One popular modality is acupuncture, an ancient Chinese practice that involves inserting thin needles into specific points on the body to restore balance and promote healing. Acupuncture stimulates the body's natural healing mechanisms and can be effective for various conditions, including pain management, stress reduction, and digestive disorders.

Another alternative therapy gaining popularity is chiropractic care, which focuses on the spine and nervous system to optimize health and wellness. Chiropractors use spinal adjustments and manipulations to correct misalignments and improve nerve function, addressing back pain, headaches, and joint problems. Many people find relief and improved mobility through regular chiropractic treatments.

Massage therapy is another physical healing modality that offers numerous benefits for the body and mind. Massage techniques vary widely but often involve applying pressure and kneading motions to muscles and soft tissues to reduce tension, promote relaxation, and enhance circulation. Regular massage sessions can help alleviate muscle soreness, improve flexibility, and relieve stress and anxiety.

In recent years, holistic modalities like yoga and Tai Chi have gained popularity for their ability to promote physical health and emotional well-being. These mind-body practices combine gentle movements, breathwork, and meditation to cultivate strength, flexibility, and inner peace. Yoga, in particular, has been shown to offer numerous health benefits, including improved cardiovascular health, reduced inflammation, and enhanced mood and mental clarity.

Nutrition and dietary changes also play a crucial role in physical healing. Our foods provide essential nutrients and energy for our bodies to function optimally. Adopting a balanced and nutritious diet can support overall health and vitality while avoiding processed foods and excessive sugar and salt intake can help prevent chronic diseases and promote longevity. Many also benefit from dietary supplements and herbal remedies to address specific health concerns and deficiencies.

Physical healing modalities offer a plethora of options for individuals like you, who are seeking to improve their health and well-being. Whether you lean towards conventional medicine, alternative therapies, or a combination of both, the power of choice is in your hands. By listening to your body and exploring what works best for you, you can take a proactive approach to your health. Incorporating these healing practices into your lifestyle can support your body's natural ability to heal and thrive, putting you in control of your well-being.

6.2 Emotional healing techniques

Emotional healing techniques are essential for addressing the inner wounds and traumas that affect our mental and psychological well-being. These techniques focus on processing and releasing negative emotions, fostering self-awareness and acceptance, and cultivating emotional resilience and balance. Here are some effective emotional healing techniques that can help you navigate through challenging times and promote emotional well-being:

Therapeutic counseling

Talking to a therapist or counselor can provide a safe and supportive space to explore and process your emotions. Therapists use various techniques such as cognitive-behavioral therapy (CBT), dialectical behavior therapy (DBT), and mindfulness-based approaches to help you understand your feelings, identify unhealthy patterns, and develop coping strategies.

Journaling

Writing down your thoughts and feelings in a journal can be a powerful tool for emotional healing. Journaling allows you to express yourself freely, gain insights into your emotions, and track your progress over time. You can use your journal to reflect on past experiences, set intentions for the future, and practice gratitude and self-compassion.

Mindfulness and meditation

Mindfulness practices involve paying attention to the present moment with openness and non-judgment. Meditation techniques, such as focused breathing or body scan, can help calm the mind, reduce stress and anxiety, and increase self-awareness. Regular mindfulness can enhance emotional regulation and resilience, allowing you to respond more skillfully to difficult emotions.

Emotional release exercises

Physical activities like dancing, yoga, or martial arts can help release pent-up emotions stored in the body. These practices encourage movement and expression, allowing you to release tension and connect with your feelings in a safe and supportive environment. You can also try techniques like shaking, deep breathing, or vocalizing to release emotional energy.

Art therapy

Engaging in creative activities such as painting, drawing, or sculpting can be therapeutic for processing emotions and exploring your inner world. Art therapy allows you to express yourself nonverbally, tap into your subconscious mind, and gain insights into your emotional state. You don't need to be an artist to benefit from art therapy—the focus is on the process rather than the final product.

Self-compassion practices

Cultivating self-compassion involves treating yourself with kindness, understanding, and acceptance, especially during challenging times. You can practice self-compassion by offering yourself words of encouragement, comforting gestures, or acts of self-care. A compassionate attitude towards yourself can help soothe difficult emotions and build strength and resilience.

Energy healing modalities

Techniques like Reiki, acupuncture, or energy psychology balance the body's energy systems to promote emotional and physical well-being. These modalities work on the principle that the body's energy flow disruptions can manifest as emotional or physical symptoms. By restoring balance to the energy system, these practices can help alleviate emotional distress and promote healing.

Trauma-informed approaches

For individuals with a history of trauma, trauma-informed approaches such as somatic experiencing or EMDR (Eye Movement Desensitization and Reprocessing) can be particularly beneficial. These techniques focus on processing and integrating traumatic memories stored in the body, allowing for healing and resolution of past wounds.

Supportive relationships

Building and nurturing supportive relationships with friends, family, or support groups can provide valuable emotional support and validation. Connecting with others who understand and empathize with your experiences can help you feel less alone and more understood. Sharing your thoughts and feelings with trusted individuals can offer perspective and insight into your emotions.

Self-care practices

Regular self-care activities such as exercise, healthy eating, adequate sleep, and relaxation techniques are essential for maintaining emotional well-being. Taking care of your physical and emotional needs can help prevent burnout, reduce stress, and increase resilience in life's challenges.

Emotional healing techniques offer valuable tools for processing emotions, resolving inner conflicts, and promoting emotional well-being. By incorporating these practices into your daily life and seeking support, you can develop greater emotional resilience, self-awareness, and inner peace. Remember that healing is a journey, and seeking help and support along the way is okay.

6.3 Spiritual healing practices

Spiritual healing practices include a wide variety of methods and approaches aimed at restoring harmony and balance to the mind, body, and spirit. The idea that one's physical and emotional health are inextricably linked to one's spiritual well-being is the foundation upon which these practices are built. Those who take the time to address their spiritual needs and establish a connection with a higher power or their inner knowledge have the potential to undergo great healing and transformation.

6.3.1 Connecting with Higher Power

One essential part of spiritual healing is connecting with a higher power or heavenly source of guidance and assistance. Many people consider this greater force God, the universe, or a spiritual presence beyond human comprehension. Prayer, meditation, and contemplation may help you develop your connection while seeking direction, strength, and comfort during difficult times.

Prayer is a powerful spiritual activity in which you communicate with the divine via spoken or silent words. Prayer, whether recited traditionally, expressed personally, or engaged in spontaneous communication with a higher power, may build a sense of connection, thankfulness, and faith in the divine purpose. Through prayer, people can express their concerns, aspirations, and goals to a higher power, finding comfort in knowing they are not alone in their challenges.

Meditation is another spiritual activity that helps people connect with their inner selves and the divine. It quiets the mind, focuses on the present moment, and fosters inner stillness, helping people achieve a deeper feeling of calm, clarity, and spiritual understanding. Meditation, whether via mindfulness, guided imagery, or mantra repetition, can assist individuals in connecting with their spiritual nature and aligning with the divine presence inside and around them.

6.3.2 Cultivate spiritual awareness

Rituals and rituals are effective spiritual instruments for promoting healing, change, and spiritual development. These sacred rituals frequently incorporate symbolic activities, holy symbols, and communal involvement, providing a space for spiritual experience and collective healing. Individuals can use ritual healing to release the past, invoke blessings, and declare wishes for the future, whether via religious ceremonies, spiritual rituals, or personal rites of passage.

Religious ceremonies, such as Mass, prayer sessions, and sacramental rites, are essential to many spiritual traditions because they allow for community worship, meditation, and spiritual contact. These holy meetings foster a sense of belonging, solidarity, and reverence, allowing people to connect with the divine presence while receiving spiritual sustenance and grace.

Spiritual rituals, such as healing, cleansing, and empowerment ceremonies, are frequently tailored to specific needs and objectives. Depending on cultural customs and personal preferences, these rituals may include smudging, chanting, drumming, or visualization. Individuals who engage in these sacred rituals with intention and reverence can harness the healing power of ritual to release negative energy, invoke spiritual protection, and align with divine direction.

Personal rites of passage, such as vision quests, initiation ceremonies, and life transition rituals, are crucial milestones in a person's spiritual path that allow for development, change, and self-discovery. These rituals frequently include symbolic activities, storytelling, and communal support, allowing people to reflect on their history, appreciate the present, and envisage their future. Individuals reverently and intentionally recognize these holy transformations may negotiate life's changes with grace, wisdom, and resilience.

6.4 Integrative treatment approaches

Integrative therapy approaches combine treatments and strategies from diverse therapeutic traditions to address individuals' overall needs. These techniques emphasize that healing encompasses the linked parts of mind, body, and spirit and aim to combine complementary activities for maximum wellbeing.

Integrative healing is a comprehensive approach to wellbeing that considers health's physical, emotional, mental, and spiritual aspects. Rather than concentrating on symptoms or isolated components of a person's experience, integrative techniques seek to address the root causes of imbalance and enhance overall vitality and resilience. Integrative healing acknowledges the interdependence of body, mind, and spirit by treating the entire person rather than simply the sickness or affliction.

Integrative healing incorporates both Eastern and Western healing traditions, acknowledging the value of each method. Eastern techniques such as acupuncture, yoga, and Ayurveda provide ancient wisdom and practices that improve bodily harmony, balance, and energy flow. These techniques aim to restore the body's natural healing mechanisms and correct imbalances in the subtle energy systems.

Conventional medicine, psychotherapy, and nutritional counseling are Western therapies that use evidence to diagnose, treat, and prevent illness. These techniques include scientific rigor and technology developments that add to integrative healing's holistic approach. Integrating Eastern and Western modalities provides individuals access to various tools and strategies for boosting health and wellbeing.

Integrative healing emphasizes individualized treatment regimens adapted to each person's requirements, preferences, and goals. Rather than using a one-size-fits-all strategy, integrative practitioners work with clients to build personalized techniques for dealing with their particular health challenges. This tailored approach may include a variety of therapy modalities, lifestyle changes, and self-care behaviors that encourage patients to participate actively in their recovery process.

Integrative healing acknowledges the interdependence of the mind, body, and spirit and strives for harmony and balance in all parts of life. Meditation, mindfulness, and expressive arts therapy promote awareness, presence, and self-expression, which aids in healing on various levels. Integrative healing enables people to tap into their intrinsic healing resources and build a more incredible feeling of wellbeing and energy by fostering the mind-body-spirit link.

Chapter 7: Develop self-compassion

This chapter delves into the transformative power of self-compassion, a vital component of emotional well-being and personal growth. Self-compassion involves treating ourselves with the same kindness and understanding that we would offer to a close friend in times of struggle or difficulty. By exploring self-compassion principles and practices, we aim to foster greater self-acceptance, resilience, and inner peace. Join us on this journey of self-discovery and learn how to cultivate a compassionate relationship with yourself.

7.1 What is self-compassion?

Self-compassion is like giving yourself a warm hug when life gets tough. It's about being kind and understanding, especially when facing challenges or feeling down. Think about how you'd comfort a friend going through a hard time – that's the compassion you want to show yourself.

Self-compassion isn't about being self-indulgent or letting yourself off the hook when you make mistakes. It's the opposite. It's about acknowledging your humanity and recognizing that everyone sometimes makes mistakes and faces struggles. Instead of being hard on yourself, self-compassion encourages you to treat yourself with kindness and understanding, just like a good friend would.

7.1.1 The three elements of self-compassion

Self-compassion has three main components.

Self-kindness means being gentle and understanding with yourself, especially when you're struggling. Instead of criticizing yourself for your shortcomings or failures, try offering yourself words of encouragement and support.

Common humanity: it's easy to feel like you're the only one going through a tough time, but the truth is, everyone faces challenges in life. Recognizing that suffering is a natural part of the human experience can help you feel less isolated and more connected to others.

Mindfulness: being mindful means being aware of your thoughts and feelings without judging them as good or bad. When you practice mindfulness, you can observe your inner experiences with greater clarity and acceptance, which can help you respond to them with compassion.

7.1.2 The benefits of self-compassion

Self-compassion isn't just a feel-good concept – it's backed by research that shows it can have numerous benefits for your mental and emotional well-being. Here are some of the ways self-compassion can positively impact your life.

When your kind to yourself, you're less likely to get caught up in negative thought patterns that can increase stress and anxiety.

Self-compassionate people are better able to bounce back from setbacks and failures because they are less hard on themselves when things go wrong.

Self-compassion is linked to higher happiness, optimism, and overall life satisfaction.

When you're kinder to yourself, you're also more compassionate toward others, which can strengthen your relationships and improve your social connections.

7.1.3 Practicing self-compassion

Self-compassion is a skill that can be developed with practice. Here are some ways to cultivate self-compassion in your daily life:

Take a self-compassion break: acknowledge your suffering, remind yourself that it's a normal part of life, and offer yourself words of kindness and support.

Self-compassionate letter: write a letter as if you were writing to a dear friend struggling. Offer yourself words of encouragement and understanding.

Self-compassion meditation: practice mindfulness meditation to cultivate feelings of kindness and compassion toward yourself.

Remember, self-compassion isn't about being perfect or never making mistakes. It's about embracing your humanity with kindness and understanding and recognizing that you deserve the same compassion you would offer to anyone else.

7.2 Cultivating practices of self-compassion

So, you want to become a self-compassion pro? It's like training for a marathon – it takes practice, patience, and a lot of heart. But don't worry, I've got your back. Here are some self-compassion practices to get you started on your journey:

1) Start small

Rome wasn't built in a day, and neither is self-compassion. Start by incorporating small acts of kindness into your daily routine. Maybe it's giving yourself a pep talk when stressed or treating yourself to your favorite snack after a long day.

2) Practice mindfulness

Mindfulness is like a superpower when it comes to self-compassion. Take a few moments daily to tune into your thoughts and feelings without judgment. Notice when you're being hard on yourself and gently redirect your thoughts toward kindness and understanding.

3) Challenge your inner critic

We all have that little voice that loves to criticize us. But here's the thing – that voice isn't always right. Challenge your inner critic by questioning its validity. Would you say the same things to a friend? Probably not. Treat yourself with the same kindness and compassion you would offer to someone you care about.

4) Practice self-kindness

Treat yourself like you would a beloved friend. Offer yourself words of encouragement and support, especially when you're facing challenges or setbacks. Instead of beating yourself up for your mistakes, remind yourself that everyone messes up sometimes, and that's okay.

5) Connect with others

Sometimes, the best way to cultivate self-compassion is by connecting with others. Contact friends or family members who make you feel supported and loved. Share your struggles and allow yourself to receive their kindness and understanding.

6) Celebrate your strengths

We're often quick to focus on our weaknesses and overlook our strengths. Take time to celebrate your accomplishments and the things that make you unique. Remember, you're a work in progress, and every step forward is worth celebrating.

7) Practice gratitude

Gratitude is like fertilizer for self-compassion – it helps you grow and thrive. Take a few moments each day to reflect on the things you're grateful for, whether it's a beautiful sunset, a hot cup of coffee, or the support of loved ones.

8) Forgive yourself

Let go of past mistakes and forgive yourself for any perceived shortcomings. Remember, you're only human, and everyone makes mistakes. Instead of dwelling on the past, focus on what you can do to learn and grow from your experiences.

9) Be Patient

Cultivating self-compassion is a journey, not a destination. Be patient with yourself as you navigate the ups and downs of life. Remember, it's okay to stumble along the way – what matters is that you keep moving forward with kindness and compassion.

7.3 Overcoming obstacles to self-compassion

In principle, self-compassion is a beautiful concept; nevertheless, let's face it: there are times when it is easier to say than practice. Every one of us is confronted with obstacles that might make it difficult to engage in self-compassion practices. Fear not, however! You can overcome these obstacles and accept the compassion and understanding you are entitled to with only a little awareness and effort.

7.3.1 Crippling self-criticism

Ah, the inner critic – that pesky voice that loves to tear us down at every turn. Self-criticism is like a relentless bully, reminding us of our faults and failures. But here's the thing – that voice isn't telling the whole truth. Challenge your inner critic by questioning its validity. Would you say the same things to a friend? Probably not. Treat yourself with the same kindness and compassion you would offer to someone you care about.

7.3.2 Fear of self-indulgence

Self-compassion often gets a bad rap for being selfish or indulgent. We're taught to put others first and prioritize their needs above our own. But here's the truth – you can't pour from an empty cup. Taking care of yourself isn't selfish – it's necessary for your well-being. Remember, practicing self-compassion isn't about neglecting your responsibilities or ignoring the needs of others. It's about treating yourself with the same kindness and understanding you would offer to a friend.

7.3.3 Cultural and social pressures

In a society that values productivity and achievement above all else, self-compassion can feel like a radical act of rebellion. We're bombarded with messages that tell us we need to be constantly striving for more – more success, more wealth, more perfection. But here's the truth – you are enough, just as you are. You don't need to earn your worth through achievement or success. Embrace the messy, imperfect, beautifully human parts of yourself, and know that you are worthy of love and compassion just as you are.

7.3.4 Past trauma and conditioning

For many of us, the barriers to self-compassion run deep, rooted in past trauma and conditioning. Maybe you grew up in an environment where vulnerability was seen as weakness, or you experienced trauma that left you feeling unworthy of love and kindness. Whatever your past experiences, know that they do not define you. You can rewrite your story and embrace a new narrative of compassion and self-love. Seek support from trusted friends, family members, or mental health professionals who can help you navigate the complexities of your past and cultivate a greater sense of compassion for yourself. Remember, healing is possible, and you are worthy of love and kindness just as you are.

7.4 Apply self-compassion in daily life

Embodying self-compassion as part of your everyday routine does not have to be challenging to do. The following are some basic ways that can assist you in incorporating self-compassion into your day-to-day life:

Begin by cultivating a heightened awareness of your thoughts and emotions during the day. Start by noticing when your inner critic begins to speak up. Then, try to identify when you are too critical of yourself. The first step toward transformation is just being conscious of the conversation that takes place inside you.

You should make it a habit to interact with yourself with the same compassion and understanding you would provide to a close friend. Respond with kindness rather than condemnation when you find yourself in a situation where you have failed to meet your standards or made a mistake. Remember that nobody is flawless, and it is perfectly OK to be kind to yourself, regardless of your gender, age, or background.

It is essential to include mindfulness in your everyday practice. Pause for a few seconds and check in with yourself occasionally. Consider how you are experiencing on a physical, emotional, and cerebral level without passing judgment on your experiences. The practice of mindfulness may assist you in being more self-aware of your requirements and respond to them with compassion.

It's important to acknowledge and accept your emotions, even the challenging ones. Remember, it's normal to feel a range of emotions, and they are all valid. Recognize that your feelings are real and a normal part of the human experience, rather than passing judgment on yourself whenever you experience a certain emotion.

Take the time to learn how to establish boundaries and prioritize your needs and well-being. It is not a bad idea to decline an offer and prioritize your needs. Remember that you can't pour from an empty cup, so make sure that you prioritize taking care of yourself.

Rejoice in your accomplishments and victories, no matter how little they seem. Take the time to recognize and rejoice in your accomplishments rather than concentrating entirely on what you have not done well. Every achievement, regardless of how little it may seem, deserves acknowledgment.

Remember, it's okay to ask for help when you need it. If you're feeling overwhelmed or struggling, don't hesitate to reach out to friends, family, or mental health professionals. Having a strong support system can make a world of difference in cultivating more self-compassion and navigating challenging emotions.

Develop an attitude of thankfulness by setting aside some time every day to think about the things for which you are grateful. The practice of gratitude may foster a better feeling of satisfaction and self-compassion, which can assist in shifting your emphasis from what is missing in your life to what is present in your life.

Finally, let go of self-blame and engage in the practice of forgiving others. Self-blame is when we hold ourselves responsible for something that went wrong, even if it was out of our control. Remember that nobody is flawless and that we all go through periods of life in which we make errors. Instead of ruminating on the mistakes you've made in the past, you should concentrate on going ahead with compassion and care toward yourself.

Chapter 8: Overcoming adult challenges with the inner child

8.1 Comprehending the influence of the inner child

Our inner child holds significant sway over our emotions, thoughts, and behaviors, often shaping how we navigate the complexities of adulthood. Understanding this influence is crucial for our personal growth and emotional well-being. Here's why:

Roots in childhood experiences

The inner child represents the emotional and psychological imprint of our childhood experiences. These formative years lay the foundation for our beliefs about ourselves, others, and the world. Positive experiences can foster resilience and confidence, while negative ones may lead to deep-seated insecurities and emotional wounds.

Impact on adult life

Although we may not always be aware, the inner child influences our perceptions and responses to present-day situations. Unresolved issues from childhood can manifest in various ways, such as fear of abandonment, seeking validation from others, or struggling with self-worth. These patterns often affect our relationships, career choices, and overall well-being.

Triggers and emotional reactions

Certain events or interactions can trigger strong emotional reactions that seem disproportionate to the current situation. These reactions often stem from unhealed wounds of the inner child. For example, criticism from a colleague may evoke feelings of inadequacy reminiscent of childhood experiences of being criticized or belittled.

Repetition of patterns

Without conscious awareness and intervention, individuals may repeat negative patterns or behaviors learned in childhood. These patterns can sabotage personal and professional relationships, hinder career advancement, and contribute to feelings of stagnation or unhappiness.

Limiting beliefs and self-sabotage

The inner child holds onto beliefs formed in response to past experiences, even if they no longer serve us in adulthood. These limiting beliefs may include notions of unworthiness, fear of failure, or the need to please others constantly. Such beliefs can perpetuate self-sabotaging behaviors and prevent us from reaching our full potential.

Healing and integration

Recognizing the influence of the inner child is the first step toward healing and integration. By acknowledging and validating the emotions and experiences of our inner child, we can begin the process of healing past wounds and rewriting the narratives that no longer serve us. This journey of self-discovery and healing allows us to reclaim our authenticity, resilience, and inner joy.

Understanding the influence of the inner child empowers us to cultivate greater self-awareness, compassion, and emotional resilience in our adult lives. By nurturing and healing our inner child, we can create a solid foundation for personal growth, meaningful relationships, and a fulfilling life journey.

8.2 Healing the wounds of the childhood past

Navigating adulthood often means confronting the lingering wounds and traumas from our childhood. While these experiences may have shaped us, they don't have to define us. Healing past wounds from childhood is a transformative journey toward self-discovery and emotional liberation. Here's how to embark on this healing process:

The first step in healing past wounds is acknowledging the pain and trauma we experienced during childhood. This requires courage and vulnerability, as it may unearth buried emotions and memories. Rather than suppressing or denying our pain, we must confront it with compassion and understanding. By acknowledging our wounds, we validate our inner child's experiences and begin the journey toward healing. Forgiveness is a powerful tool in the healing process for ourselves and others.

Holding onto resentment and anger only perpetuates our suffering, while forgiveness offers the opportunity for emotional freedom and closure. This doesn't mean condoning or forgetting past wrongs but releasing their grip on our hearts and minds. Forgiveness is a gift we give ourselves, allowing us to break free from resentment and move forward with grace and compassion.

Healing past wounds from childhood often requires the guidance and support of trained professionals, such as therapists or counselors. These professionals provide a safe and supportive environment for exploring our emotions, processing traumatic experiences, and learning healthy coping strategies. Therapy offers valuable tools and techniques for healing, such as cognitive-behavioral therapy (CBT), dialectical behavior therapy (DBT), and eye movement desensitization and reprocessing (EMDR). Through therapy, we gain insight into our patterns and behaviors, develop healthier coping mechanisms, and cultivate greater self-awareness and resilience.

Practicing self-compassion and self-care is essential for healing past wounds from childhood. This involves treating ourselves with kindness, understanding, and patience as we navigate the healing journey. Self-compassion allows us to honor our pain without judgment, offering ourselves the same kindness and compassion we would extend to a loved one in need. Self-care practices, such as mindfulness, meditation, journaling, and creative expression, nurture our emotional well-being and provide a refuge for healing. By prioritizing our self-care, we replenish our emotional reserves and cultivate resilience in the face of adversity.

Central to healing past wounds from childhood is tending to the needs of our inner child—the wounded and vulnerable part of ourselves that still carries the pain of the past. This involves reconnecting with our inner child through nurturing and compassionate practices, such as inner child meditations, creative expression, and inner dialogue. By offering love, acceptance, and validation to our inner child, we create a safe space for healing and integration. Through this process, we reclaim our inner strength, resilience, and capacity for joy.

Healing past wounds from childhood is a journey of resilience and empowerment. As we confront and overcome our past challenges, we emerge stronger, wiser, and more resilient. By embracing our vulnerability and embracing the healing process, we reclaim our power and agency over our lives. This journey is not always easy, but it is profoundly transformative, leading us toward greater self-awareness, compassion, and wholeness.

8.3 Reconnect with playfulness and creativity

Rediscovering the joy of playfulness and creativity is essential for mending our inner child and facing adulthood's problems with a fresh perspective. Here's how you can reconnect with your fun and creative side.

Rediscover the freedom of spontaneity by allowing oneself to participate in things only for their enjoyment, without regard for the outcome or production. Whether sketching in a notebook, dancing around your living room, or making a blanket fort, enjoy the moment's spontaneity and let your inner kid lead the way.

Unleash your inner creativity by exploring different artistic outlets that appeal to you. Whether you enjoy painting, writing, singing, or creating, seek out hobbies that enable you to express yourself freely and genuinely. Make time for creative play and exploration, allowing oneself to explore without judgment or criticism.

Do things that make you happy and giggle to add moments of playfulness to your life. This might be playing a game with friends, taking a bike trip, or spending time outside in nature. Allow yourself to be completely present in the moment, experiencing the childish wonder and curiosity that accompany joyful pursuits.

Cultivate your imagination by immersing yourself in tales, novels, movies, and other sources of creative inspiration. Allow your mind to go wild, discovering new worlds and possibilities outside the confines of daily existence. Accept the enchantment of storytelling and creation to reconnect with your inner child's sense of wonder and fantasy.

Cultivate mindfulness and presence in your daily life by paying attention to the present moment with curiosity and openness. Please take a moment to appreciate the beauty and wonder around you, whether it's the colors of a sunset, the sound of birds chirping, or the sensation of a soft wind on your skin. By practicing mindfulness, you may better appreciate life's tiny delights and pleasures, reconnecting with your inner child's feelings of surprise and amazement.

Share fun moments with friends, family, and loved ones to foster connection and camaraderie. Set up game evenings, creative workshops, or outdoor trips where you can laugh, play, and connect with people meaningfully. You may build lasting memories and strengthen your bonds with people by instilling a feeling of fun and delight in your interactions.

8.4 Embrace vulnerability and authenticity

Embracing vulnerability and authenticity is key to healing past wounds from childhood and fostering deeper connections in adulthood. Here's how you can cultivate vulnerability and authenticity in your life

Start by acknowledging and accepting your emotions, even the ones that feel uncomfortable or difficult. Allow yourself to sit with these feelings without judgment or criticism, recognizing that vulnerability is a natural and essential part of the human experience.

Practice speaking your truth and sharing your authentic self with others. Be honest about your thoughts, feelings, and experiences, even if they feel scary or vulnerable. Being open and transparent with those around you can cultivate deeper connections and build trust in your relationships.

Establishing healthy boundaries is crucial for protecting your emotional well-being and honoring your authentic self. Learn to say no to things that don't align with your values or priorities and communicate your boundaries clearly and assertively to others. Setting boundaries allows you to protect your energy and maintain a sense of authenticity in your interactions with others.

Be kind and compassionate toward yourself, especially during times of vulnerability or struggle. Treat yourself with the same warmth and understanding you would offer a dear friend, and practice self-care activities that nourish your mind, body, and soul. Cultivating self-compassion helps you to embrace your imperfections and vulnerabilities with greater acceptance and love.

Don't be afraid to seek support from trusted friends, family members, or mental health professionals when you're feeling vulnerable or overwhelmed. Surround yourself with people who accept you for who you are and offer unconditional love and support. Sharing your struggles with others can help you feel less alone and more connected to those around you.

Strive to live authentically by aligning your actions with your values, beliefs, and desires. Be true to yourself in all areas of your life, whether in your relationships, career, or personal pursuits. Authenticity involves being genuine and honest with yourself and others, even when it feels uncomfortable or challenging.

Let go of the need to be perfect and embrace your imperfections as part of what makes you uniquely human. Accept that you are a work in progress and that growth often comes through vulnerability and mistakes. You can cultivate a greater sense of self-compassion and authenticity by embracing your imperfections.

8.5 Building resilience and self-compassion

Building resilience and self-compassion is essential for navigating life's challenges with an inner child perspective. Here are some practical strategies to help you cultivate resilience and self-compassion

1) Developing a growth mindset

Cultivate a growth mindset by reframing challenges as opportunities for growth and learning. Instead of viewing setbacks as failures, see them as valuable lessons to help you become stronger and more resilient. Embrace the belief that you have the power to overcome obstacles and learn from adversity.

2) Practicing self-compassion

Treat yourself with kindness and compassion, especially during difficult times. Practice self-care activities that nourish your mind, body, and soul, such as meditation, exercise, or time in nature. Be gentle with yourself and offer yourself the same love and support you would give a close friend.

3) Cultivating emotional awareness

Develop greater awareness of your emotions and learn healthy coping methods. Instead of suppressing or ignoring your feelings, acknowledge them and allow yourself to experience them fully. Practice mindfulness techniques like deep breathing or body scanning to help you stay present and grounded amid challenging emotions.

4) Building supportive relationships

Surround yourself with supportive friends, family members, and mentors who uplift and encourage you. Cultivate deep, meaningful connections with others who accept you for who you are and offer unconditional love and support. Lean on your support network during times of need and be willing to provide support to others in return.

5) Setting realistic goals

Set realistic goals for yourself and take small, manageable steps toward achieving them. Break larger goals down into smaller, more achievable tasks, and celebrate your progress along the way. Setting realistic goals and taking consistent action can build confidence and resilience in the face of challenges.

6) Practicing gratitude

Cultivate an attitude of gratitude by focusing on the positive aspects of your life, even during difficult times. Take time each day to reflect on what you're grateful for, whether it's your health, relationships, or simple pleasures like a beautiful sunset. Practicing gratitude can help shift your perspective and foster resilience in adversity.

7) Learning from failure

Embrace failure as an inevitable part of the learning process and an opportunity for growth. Instead of dwelling on past mistakes or setbacks, reflect on what you can learn from them and how to improve. Failure is not a reflection of your worth but a natural part of the journey toward success.

If you're struggling to cope with life's challenges alone, don't hesitate to seek professional support. A therapist or counselor can provide guidance, support, and practical tools to help you navigate difficult emotions and build resilience. There's no shame in asking for help when needed, and reaching out for support is a courageous act of self-care.

Chapter 9: Overcoming the illusion of control

9.1 The nature of control

Control is like attempting to hold onto a fistful of sand in the larger scheme of things: the tighter you grab, the more it slides between your fingers. This is because control is frequently an illusion, a mirage that leads us to believe we have complete control over everything. But the truth is that life is unpredictable, and several factors are outside our control. Understanding the nature of control is the first step in handling this complicated and sometimes challenging part of human existence.

Control comes in several flavors. There's the type of control we have over our behaviors and decisions, which psychologists term "internal control." This is when we make decisions and perform acts that affect our lives and the world around us. For example, choosing to consume nutritious foods or going for a run are choices we make to manage our health and well-being.

Then there's external control, which refers to the urge to affect or manage the environment around us. This is where things become complicated because, while we may have some influence on external events, we will never entirely control them. Things beyond our control include weather patterns, other people's actions, and world events.

Fear of uncertainty or a need for security are common motivations for wanting control. We want to feel like we have control over things because it gives us a sense of security and stability. But the truth is that life is essentially unpredictable, and attempting to control everything only causes tension, worry, and dissatisfaction.

Another component of control is the differentiation between good and harmful control. Healthy control is accepting responsibility for our lives, making educated decisions, and establishing limits. On the other hand, unhealthy control is defined by rigid thinking, perfectionism, and a need to micromanage every element of life.

The sense of control is just that—a delusion. No matter how much we plan, plot, or attempt to influence our circumstances, there will always be variables beyond our control. Learning to embrace this fact is the first step in breaking free from the captivity of the illusion of control.

But this does not imply we are helpless. While we cannot influence external circumstances, we can choose how we react. We may nurture resilience, flexibility, and mindfulness, which will help us negotiate life's ups and downs with grace and tranquility.

Ultimately, the secret to overcoming the illusion of control is to embrace uncertainty, let go of attachment to results, and submit to life's natural flow. It's about finding calm amid turmoil and learning to dance to the unexpected beat of life.

9.2 The pitfalls of trying to control everything

Trying to manage everything is like attempting to hold onto many helium balloons in a hurricane; it's a formula for catastrophe. While it is customary to desire to feel in control of our lives, the fact is that the more we want to govern, the more out of control we typically think. Let's look at some of the most prevalent hazards of managing everything.

First and foremost, attempting to keep everything under control is taxing. It's like playing a never-ending game of whack-a-mole: when you think you've got one issue under control, five more appear in its place. The continual urge to micromanage every area of life leaves us exhausted, frustrated, and stressed.

Trying to manage everything is not only tiresome but also extremely restrictive. We miss life's beauty and unpredictability when solely concerned with controlling outcomes. We get so focused on keeping to our plan that we miss out on all the fantastic possibilities and surprises.

Another disadvantage of attempting to control everything is that it frequently results in feelings of frustration and disappointment. Regardless of how hard we try, things will always be beyond our control. When reality does not meet our expectations, we feel disappointed and disillusioned.

Furthermore, attempting to control everything might have a detrimental effect on our relationships. The more we try to control our partner's conduct, children's choices, or friends' viewpoints, the more we drive them away. People dislike feeling manipulated or micromanaged; attempting to dominate them only causes anger and conflict.

But maybe the most serious disadvantage of attempting to control everything is that it is eventually ineffective. Life is unpredictable and ever-changing, and no amount of planning or thinking will alter that. Trying to manage everything is like trying to stop the flood; it's a war we're sure to lose.

So, what are the alternatives? Instead of attempting to control everything, we might accept life's flow. We may learn to accept uncertainty, let go of our attachment to results, and believe in the universe's innate wisdom. This does not suggest that we abandon our aims or stop taking action; rather, we release our hold and allow life to develop spontaneously.

By letting go of the impulse to control everything, we open ourselves up to new possibilities. We grow more flexible, adaptive, and robust when faced with inevitable ups and downs. We learn to trust our own abilities and the cosmos to guide us on our journey.

Attempting to control everything is ultimately futile. It depletes our energy, inhibits our ability, and eventually leaves us disappointed and disillusioned. Instead of clinging to the illusion of control, let us learn to submit to the flow of life and believe that everything is going precisely as it should.

9.3 Acceptance and renunciation

Acceptance and surrender may sound like giving up or admitting defeat, yet they are effective strategies for achieving peace and fulfillment in a world that is frequently beyond our control. Let's examine what acceptance and surrender actually imply and how they might assist us in transcending the illusion of control.

Acceptance begins with recognizing reality as it is, without judgment or opposition. It's about admitting, "Okay, this is how things are right now, and that's okay." Rather than wasting energy wishing things were different, acceptance helps us be at peace with the current moment and move forward with clarity and direction.

Surrender, on the other hand, entails letting go of our attachment to results and believing in the wisdom of life. It is about letting go of the impulse to control every detail and allowing things to happen organically. Surrender does not indicate giving up on our aims or desires; rather, it implies being open to new pathways and outcomes than those we had anticipated.

Acceptance and surrender are potent combinations that may help us negotiate life's ups and downs with grace and perseverance. Accepting what we cannot alter and surrendering to the flow of life relieves us of the stress of attempting to control everything and opens us to a world of possibilities.

One of the primary advantages of acceptance and surrender is that they help us create inner calm and tranquility. Instead of continually fighting reality, we learn to go with the flow and believe everything is going perfectly. This doesn't suggest that we become passive or resigned; it simply means that we stop wasting energy on futile struggle and instead concentrate our efforts on what we can control.

Acceptance and surrender build a sense of trust in ourselves and the cosmos. We are free of tension and concern when we stop attempting to force outcomes and instead believe in the natural order of things. We learn to believe in our capacities to deal with whatever life throws at us, knowing we have the power and resilience to conquer any obstacle.

Acceptance and surrender promote emotional resilience and well-being. When we stop battling reality and start accepting things as they are, we feel tremendous relief and liberty. We are no longer burdened by the desire to control everything and instead feel liberated to completely embrace life, with all of its uncertainties and flaws.

To summarize, acceptance and surrender are powerful techniques that may help us transcend the illusion of control and achieve greater peace and fulfillment. By learning to accept what we cannot alter and submitting to the flow of life, we relieve ourselves of the stress of attempting to control everything and open ourselves to a world of possibilities.

9.4 Embracing uncertainty

Embracing uncertainty can feel like stepping into the unknown, but it's also an opportunity for growth, learning, and discovery. Let's explore why embracing uncertainty can be beneficial and how we can learn to navigate it with confidence and courage.

Firstly, uncertainty is a natural part of life. No matter how much we plan and prepare, there will always be elements of unpredictability and change. Instead of fearing uncertainty, we can learn to embrace it as an ordinary and necessary aspect of the human experience. By accepting that uncertainty is inevitable, we can free ourselves from anxiety and learn to adapt and thrive in ever-changing circumstances.

Moreover, uncertainty can be a catalyst for personal growth and development. We stretch ourselves and discover new strengths and abilities when we step outside our comfort zones and embrace new challenges and opportunities. Uncertainty pushes us to think creatively, problem-solve, and adapt – skills essential for success in our personal and professional lives.

Embracing uncertainty can lead to greater resilience and emotional well-being. When we learn to tolerate uncertainty and trust in our ability to handle whatever comes our way, we build resilience and inner strength. Instead of being overwhelmed by fear and anxiety, we develop confidence and empowerment to face life's challenges with courage and grace.

Furthermore, uncertainty can open the door to new possibilities and opportunities. When we let go of the need for certainty and control, we become more open-minded and receptive to life's unexpected gifts. By embracing uncertainty, we allow ourselves to explore new paths, try new things, and embark on exciting adventures that we may never have considered otherwise.

One key to embracing uncertainty is cultivating a mindset of curiosity and openness. Instead of viewing uncertainty as something to be feared or avoided, we can approach it with wonder and excitement. By adopting a curious mindset, we can see uncertainty as an opportunity for growth and exploration rather than a threat to our security and stability.

Embracing uncertainty requires us to let go of our attachment to outcomes and trust in the process of life. Instead of trying to control every aspect of our lives, we can learn to surrender to the flow of life and trust that everything is unfolding exactly as it should. By relinquishing our need for certainty and control, we free ourselves from worry and anxiety and open ourselves to endless possibilities.

In conclusion, embracing uncertainty is a powerful practice that can lead to greater resilience, growth, and well-being. By accepting uncertainty as a natural part of life, cultivating a mindset of curiosity and openness, and trusting in the process of life, we can learn to navigate uncertainty with confidence and courage. Instead of fearing the unknown, we can embrace it as an opportunity for growth, learning, and discovery and open ourselves to a world of endless possibilities.

9.5 Letting go of perfectionism

Letting go of perfectionism is like shedding a heavy load we've carried far too long. It's about releasing ourselves from our unreasonable expectations and making room for honesty, growth, and self-care.

First and foremost, perfectionism is frequently motivated by a fear of failure or rejection. We may feel that until we are flawless, we are unworthy of love, respect, or success. This dread might motivate us to strive for unreachable goals and make unrealistic expectations for ourselves. However, perfection is an illusion; no one is perfect, and aiming for it only leads to dissatisfaction, worry, and fatigue.

Perfectionism might prevent us from taking chances and achieving our objectives and ambitions. When we continuously aim for perfection, we become immobilized by fear of failure and refuse to venture outside of our comfort zones. We may ignore challenges or possibilities for growth and achievement because we are fearful of not meeting our unreasonable expectations.

Additionally, perfectionism can harm our relationships and mental health. When we seek perfection from ourselves, we frequently push the same standards on others, resulting in tension, conflict, and disappointment. Perfectionism may also lead to anxiety, melancholy, and low self-esteem as we strive to fulfill our unachievable standards and continuously judge ourselves for falling short.

Letting up of perfectionism does not imply settling for mediocrity or abandoning our aims and aspirations. Instead, it is about pursuing greatness while accepting imperfection and learning from our failures. It is about accepting that failure does not reflect our value as individuals but rather a chance for growth and self-discovery.

Self-compassion is an essential step in letting go of perfectionism. Instead of blaming ourselves for our flaws and failures, we may treat ourselves with the same care and understanding we would provide to a friend. With inquiry and compassion, we may recognize our humanity, celebrate our achievements, and learn from our failings.

Furthermore, letting up perfectionism necessitates rethinking our attitudes and ideas about success and failure. Instead of perceiving success as the absence of failure or mistakes, we might reframe it as the desire to take chances, learn from our experiences, and evolve as people. By adopting a growth mindset, we may regard failure as a normal part of the learning process and a chance for personal growth and development.

Letting go of perfectionism is a liberating and inspiring process that allows us to accept our authenticity, develop self-compassion, and pursue our objectives with bravery and perseverance. By freeing ourselves from the grasp of perfectionism, we allow ourselves to live wholly and truthfully, embracing our flaws and appreciating our unique skills and abilities.

9.6 Finding freedom in non-attachment

Finding freedom in non-attachment is like learning to dance gracefully with the ebb and flow of life's currents. It's about letting go of our attachment to outcomes, possessions, and even our sense of identity, allowing us to experience true liberation and inner peace.

9.6.1 Understanding non-attachment

Non-attachment is not about indifference or detachment from life; instead, it's about embracing life fully while remaining unattached to specific outcomes or circumstances. It's about recognizing that everything in life is impermanent and ever-changing, and clinging to things or experiences only leads to suffering. Non-attachment allows us to appreciate the beauty of life without being bound by our desires or fears.

9.6.2 Embracing impermanence

Central to the practice of non-attachment is the recognition of impermanence—the understanding that everything in life is transient and fleeting. This includes not only material possessions but also our thoughts, emotions, and relationships. When we cling to things or people, we inevitably experience disappointment and sorrow when they change or leave our lives. However, by embracing impermanence and letting go of our attachments, we can find freedom and peace amidst life's constant flux.

9.6.3 Living with openness and acceptance

Non-attachment invites us to live with openness and acceptance, allowing life to unfold naturally without trying to control or manipulate outcomes. It's about surrendering to the present moment, whatever it may bring, and trusting in the universe's wisdom. We free ourselves from worry and anxiety when we release our attachment to specific outcomes or expectations. Instead, we can fully engage with life with curiosity, wonder, and gratitude.

Non-attachment encourages us to cultivate a sense of detachment from our ego – the false sense of self based on our roles, achievements, and possessions. When we identify too closely with our ego, we become caught up in the illusion of separateness and lose sight of our interconnectedness with all beings. However, by letting go of our attachment to our ego and embracing our true essence – the pure awareness and consciousness that lies beyond the ego – we can experience a profound sense of unity and wholeness.

Finding freedom in non-attachment is a transformative journey that invites us to let go of our attachments and embrace life's impermanent and ever-changing nature. By releasing our grip on outcomes, possessions, and even our sense of identity, we can experience true liberation and inner peace. Non-attachment allows us to live with openness and acceptance, trusting in the universe's wisdom and surrendering to the flow of life with grace and ease.

Chapter 10: Service and Healing

10.1 The healing power of service

The healing power of service is like a secret elixir for the soul, offering both giver and receiver a dose of rejuvenation and renewal. When we extend ourselves to others in acts of kindness, compassion, and generosity, something profound happens within us. It's like a ripple effect, spreading warmth and light to everyone it touches.

Service isn't just about helping others; it's also about helping ourselves. It shifts our focus away from our problems and concerns, allowing us to gain perspective and a sense of purpose. You might be thinking, 'But I don't have the time or resources to engage in service.' Remember, service doesn't always have to be a grand gesture. Even small acts of kindness, like holding the door for someone or offering a smile, can make a difference. Seeing our actions' impact on someone else's life fills us with a sense of fulfillment and contentment that money can't buy.

Think about the times you've volunteered at a local shelter, helped a friend in need, or simply offered a listening ear to someone struggling. Didn't it make you feel good inside? That feeling of warmth and connection is the healing power of service at work.

Service is also a powerful antidote to the stresses and strains of modern life. In a chaotic and overwhelming world, taking the time to help others can be incredibly grounding. It not only reminds us of what truly matters and allows us to reconnect with our humanity, but it also has long-term benefits for our mental health and overall life satisfaction.

Moreover, service can break down barriers and create a sense of belonging. When we work towards a common goal, whether building homes for the homeless or cleaning up a local park, we form bonds that transcend our differences. Service can unite us in our shared humanity in a society that often feels divided, making us feel connected and valued.

However, perhaps the most profound aspect of service is its ability to heal the heart's wounds. We offer a balm to the soul when we reach out to others in love and compassion. It reminds us that we are not alone but part of something greater than ourselves. But remember, just as we need to take care of others, we also need to take care of ourselves. Self-care is an essential part of service, ensuring that we have the energy and emotional capacity to continue helping others.

Service also has a way of putting our struggles into perspective. When we see the challenges that others face, it helps us to appreciate all the blessings in our own lives. It's a humbling reminder that no matter how difficult things may seem, someone else always faces far more significant challenges, fostering a sense of gratitude and appreciation.

The healing power of service lies in its ability to connect us with ourselves, others, and something greater than ourselves. This 'something greater' can be a higher power, a collective consciousness, or simply the idea that our actions have a ripple effect that extends beyond our immediate sphere. It reminds us that we are all interconnected and that we all have a role to play in making the world a better place. And in that realization lies the true magic of service.

10.2 Types of service

When it comes to service, there's no one-size-fits-all approach. Service comes in many shapes and forms, each with its unique benefits and opportunities for growth. Here are some common types of services that you can explore.

Community service

This service involves volunteering your time and energy to help improve your local community. It could be anything from participating in a neighborhood clean-up event to volunteering at a local food bank or homeless shelter. Community service allows you to directly impact the lives of those around you and contribute to the well-being of your community.

Humanitarian aid

Humanitarian aid involves assisting people in need, often in response to natural disasters, conflicts, or other emergencies. This could include volunteering with organizations like the Red Cross or Doctors Without Borders or donating money or supplies to support relief efforts. Humanitarian aid allows you to make a difference on a global scale and help those who are most vulnerable.

Mentoring and tutoring

Mentoring and tutoring involve providing guidance and support to individuals needing help reaching their full potential. This could include tutoring students in subjects like math or reading or mentoring young people who are facing challenges in their personal or academic lives. Mentoring and tutoring allow you to share your knowledge and experience with others and positively impact their lives.

Environmental conservation

Environmental conservation involves taking action to protect and preserve the natural world. This could include volunteering with organizations that clean up beaches or parks, participating in tree-planting initiatives, or advocating for sustainability policies. Environmental conservation allows you to protect the planet for future generations and ensure that natural resources are preserved for all to enjoy.

Advocacy and activism

Advocacy and activism involve speaking out on behalf of others and working to create positive social change. This could include advocating for policies that support marginalized communities, participating in protests or demonstrations, or raising awareness about important issues through social media or community organizing. Advocacy and activism allow you to use your voice to make a difference and stand up for what you believe in.

Volunteering with animals

Volunteering with animals involves working with organizations that care for and protect animals in need. This could include volunteering at animal shelters or wildlife rehabilitation centers, fostering animals needing temporary homes, or participating in conservation efforts to protect endangered species. Volunteering with animals allows you to make a difference in the lives of great and small creatures and promote their welfare and well-being.

No matter which type of service you choose, the important thing is to find something that resonates with you and allows you to make a meaningful contribution to the world around you. Whether you're helping people, animals, or the environment, every act of service has the power to make a difference and create positive change.

10.3 Service benefits

Serving others is often seen as noble and selfless, but it's essential to recognize that service also brings significant benefits to those who serve. Engaging in acts of service can transform your life in many positive ways, offering emotional, mental, and even physical advantages. Here's a closer look at the numerous benefits of service.

Service provides a profound sense of purpose and fulfillment. When you help others, you become part of something larger than yourself. This feeling of contributing to the greater good can fill your life with meaning, which is essential for overall happiness. Knowing that your actions have positively impacted others can be incredibly rewarding and boost your self-esteem.

Service also strengthens your connection to the community. Volunteering and helping others often bring you into contact with people from diverse backgrounds, fostering a sense of unity and understanding. These interactions can broaden your perspective, allowing you to appreciate different walks of life and build empathy. Additionally, the relationships you form through service can lead to lasting friendships and a strong support network.

Engaging in service can significantly enhance your mental and emotional well-being. Helping others often shifts your focus away from your problems, which can be a refreshing break from stress and anxiety. This change in focus can lead to reduced stress levels and improved mental health. Moreover, acts of kindness trigger the release of endorphins in your brain, the so-called "helper's high," which can leave you feeling more energized and happier.

Service can be a powerful way to develop and hone skills. Whether you're organizing an event, mentoring someone, or working on a community project, you'll likely encounter new challenges requiring problem-solving and creativity. These experiences can enhance your leadership, communication, and organizational skills. Many people find that the skills they develop through service are transferable to their professional lives, giving them a competitive edge in their careers.

Physically, service can be beneficial as well. Many service forms involve physical activity, whether building homes, cleaning parks, or helping at a local food bank. These activities can keep you moving, which is excellent for your physical health. Even less strenuous service, like volunteering at a library or mentoring students, can encourage you to stay active and engaged rather than passive.

Service promotes a sense of gratitude and perspective. Seeing firsthand the challenges others face can help you appreciate what you have. This shift in perspective can foster a more positive outlook on life. By focusing on the needs of others, you become more aware of your blessings and less likely to take things for granted. This sense of gratitude can enhance your overall happiness and satisfaction with life.

Service can be an educational experience. It exposes you to different social issues and cultural practices, broadening your understanding of the world. This knowledge can empower you to become a more informed and active citizen. Understanding the complexities of social issues can also drive you to continue seeking ways to contribute and make a difference.

Lastly, service often inspires others. When people see you dedicating your time and energy to help others, it can motivate them to do the same. This ripple effect can amplify the impact of your actions, leading to a more compassionate and supportive community.

The benefits of service extend far beyond the immediate help provided to those in need. Serving others can enrich your life with purpose, strengthen your connections, improve your mental and physical health, and develop your skills. It can foster gratitude, broaden your perspective, and inspire those around you. By giving of yourself, you make the world a better place and enhance your life in countless ways.

10.4 Incorporate service into daily life

Incorporating service into daily life doesn't have to be a grand gesture; small acts of kindness and intentional efforts to help others can make a significant difference. The key is to find ways to weave service naturally into your routine, making it a regular and fulfilling part of your life. Here's how you can start:

One of the simplest ways to incorporate service is through random acts of kindness. These small, spontaneous gestures can brighten someone's day and create a ripple effect of goodwill. Smile at strangers, hold the door open for someone, or offer a compliment. These actions, though small, can have a significant impact.

Another practical approach is to volunteer regularly. Find a local organization or cause that resonates with you and commit to helping out consistently. Depending on your schedule, this could be weekly, bi-weekly, or monthly. Regular volunteering benefits the community and provides you with a sense of purpose and routine.

If you're short on time, consider micro-volunteering. This involves short, flexible activities you can do from home or in your brief free time. Examples include writing letters to isolated seniors, participating in virtual mentoring programs, or helping with online campaigns for causes you care about.

At work, look for opportunities to serve. Offer to help colleagues with projects, mentor a junior team member, or organize a charity drive. Many companies have corporate social responsibility programs where employees can volunteer during work hours. Participating in these programs can enhance workplace camaraderie and make your job more rewarding.

Get involved in local initiatives to build a sense of community in your neighborhood. Join a neighborhood watch program, help with community garden projects, or assist elderly neighbors with groceries or yard work. Being an active member of your community helps others and strengthens your sense of belonging.

Engaging in service doesn't always require a formal structure. You can incorporate it into your hobbies and interests. If you enjoy cooking, prepare extra meals for a sick friend or a needy family. If you like reading, volunteer at a local library or read to children at a nearby school. Combining your passions with service makes it enjoyable and sustainable.

Incorporate service into your family's life as well. Teach your children the value of helping others by involving them in volunteer activities. This could be as simple as baking cookies for a neighbor, participating in a charity run, or cleaning up a local park on Saturday morning. These activities can be bonding experiences and instill a sense of compassion and responsibility in your children.

Another way to serve daily is by donating regularly. Set aside a portion of your budget for charitable contributions, whether to a favorite nonprofit, a friend's fundraising campaign, or simply to someone in need. Monetary donations can substantially impact organizations, especially those relying on community support.

Don't forget the power of advocacy. Use your voice to support causes that matter to you. This can be done by signing petitions, attending rallies, or using social media to spread awareness. Being an advocate helps drive systemic change and amplifies the impact of your service.

Practice active listening and empathy. Sometimes, the best way to serve someone is by being present and truly listening to them. Offer support, lend a sympathetic ear, and show understanding. This simple act can be profoundly healing and supportive for those going through tough times.

Incorporating service into daily life is about consciously being kind, helpful, and empathetic. By finding ways to serve that align with your interests, schedule, and lifestyle, you can make a meaningful impact without feeling overwhelmed. Small, consistent acts of service can transform your life and the lives of those around you, fostering a more compassionate and connected community.

Chapter 11: Practical steps for continued healing

11.1 Establishing a daily routine for wellness

Creating a daily routine that promotes well-being is crucial for maintaining physical, emotional, and mental health. A well-structured routine can provide stability, reduce stress, and improve overall quality of life. Here are some practical steps to help you establish a daily routine for well-being.

11.1.1 Morning practices

Starting your day with intention and positive energy sets the tone for the rest of the day. One effective morning practice is to wake up at the same time each day. Consistency helps regulate your body's internal clock, making waking up and falling asleep easier.

Begin your morning with a mindfulness practice. This could be a few minutes of meditation, deep breathing exercises, or simply sitting quietly and setting your intentions for the day. Mindfulness helps center your mind, reduces anxiety, and prepares you for the day ahead.

Incorporating physical activity into your morning routine can significantly boost your mood and energy. Whether it's a brisk walk, yoga, or an entire workout session, moving your body releases endorphins and natural mood lifters. Exercise also helps increase focus and concentration, setting you up for a productive day.

11.1.2 Midday breaks

Regular breaks throughout the day are essential for maintaining productivity and mental clarity. Aim to step away from your work or daily tasks every couple of hours. Use this time to stretch, take a short walk, or simply breathe deeply.

Healthy eating habits are another vital aspect of a well-being routine. Plan your meals and snacks to nourish your body with the proper nutrients. Eating balanced meals can help maintain energy levels and prevent the afternoon slump.

Another beneficial practice is incorporating a short mindfulness or relaxation exercise during your midday break. This could be a quick meditation, listening to calming music, or engaging in a hobby you enjoy. These activities can help reduce stress and rejuvenate your mind for the rest of the day.

11.1.3 Evening wind-down

Ending your day with a consistent wind-down routine can improve the quality of your sleep and help you wake up refreshed. Establish a set bedtime that allows you to get enough sleep each night. Aim for 7-9 hours of sleep, which is the optimal range for most adults.

Create a calming evening routine that signals your body that it's time to unwind. This could include reading a book, taking a warm bath, or practicing gentle yoga or stretching. Avoid stimulating activities like using electronic devices, as the blue light emitted can interfere with your sleep cycle.

Reflecting on your day can also be a helpful practice. Spend a few minutes journaling about what went well and what you are grateful for. This reflection can foster a sense of accomplishment and positivity, making relaxing and preparing for sleep easier.

By establishing a daily routine that incorporates these morning practices, midday breaks, and evening wind-down activities, you can create a balanced and sustainable approach to well-being. This structure enhances your physical health and supports your emotional and mental resilience, helping you navigate life's challenges with greater ease and confidence.

11.2 Cultivating mindfulness and presence

Mindfulness and presence are powerful tools for enhancing your well-being and mental health. Focusing on the present moment and fully experiencing life as it happens can reduce stress, improve your emotional health, and create a deeper connection with yourself and others. Here are some practical steps to help you cultivate mindfulness and presence daily.

11.2.1 Mindfulness practices

Incorporating mindfulness practices into your routine can help you stay grounded and aware. One effective method is mindful breathing. This involves taking slow, deep breaths and paying attention to the sensation of the breath as it enters and leaves your body.

Whenever you notice your mind wandering, gently bring your focus back to your breathing. This simple practice can be done anywhere and anytime, making it a versatile tool for maintaining mindfulness throughout the day.

Another effective practice is mindful eating. This means fully engaging with the experience of eating without distractions like TV or phones. Pay attention to the colors, textures, and flavors of your food. Chew slowly and savor each bite. This enhances your enjoyment of meals and helps you become more aware of your body's hunger and fullness cues, which can improve your relationship with food and support healthier eating habits.

Mindful walking is another excellent way to cultivate presence. Instead of rushing from place to place, notice your surroundings. Feel the ground beneath your feet, listen to the sounds around you, and observe the sights and smells of your environment. This practice can transform an ordinary walk into a rich sensory experience and a moment of calm.

11.2.2 Integrating mindfulness into daily activities

Mindfulness isn't limited to formal practices; it can be integrated into almost any activity. For instance, focus on the task when doing household chores like washing dishes or folding laundry. Notice the feeling of the water on your hands, the sound of the dishes rattling, or the texture of the fabric. By bringing mindful attention to these activities, you can turn routine tasks into opportunities for presence and relaxation.

At work, take short mindfulness breaks. Close your eyes, take a few deep breaths, and focus on the present moment. This can help clear your mind, reduce stress, and improve focus and productivity. Consider setting reminders on your phone or computer to prompt you to pause and practice mindfulness throughout the day.

Mindful communication is another powerful tool. When talking with someone, could you give them your full attention? Listen actively, without planning your response or letting your mind wander. Notice their words, tone, and body language. This enhances your connections with others and helps you respond more thoughtfully and compassionately.

Cultivating mindfulness and presence is about consciously being fully engaged in the present moment, regardless of what you are doing. Integrating mindfulness practices and principles into your daily life can create a greater sense of peace, clarity, and connection. Whether through mindful breathing, eating, walking, or integrating mindfulness into everyday activities, these practices can help you navigate life's challenges with greater ease and joy.

11.3 Creating a support network

Building a solid support network is crucial for ongoing healing and well-being. Having people, you can rely on for emotional support, advice, and encouragement can make a significant difference in your life. Here are some practical steps to help you create and maintain a supportive community.

1) Start with family and friends

Your family and friends are often your first line of support. These are the people who know you best and care about you deeply. Reach out to them and tell them that you value their support. Spend quality time with them, share your experiences, and be open about your feelings. Sometimes, knowing someone is there to listen can be incredibly comforting.

2) Join a support group

Support groups are an excellent way to connect with others who are going through similar experiences. These groups provide a safe space to share your thoughts and feelings and to receive feedback and encouragement from others who understand what you're going through. Whether it's a group for mental health, addiction recovery, grief, or any other challenge, being part of a support group can help you feel less isolated and more understood.

3) Participate in community activities

Community activities can help you build new relationships and expand your support network. Consider joining clubs, volunteering, or participating in local events. These activities not only provide opportunities to meet new people but also allow you to contribute to your community, which can enhance your sense of purpose and belonging.

4) Seek professional help

Therapists, counselors, and other mental health professionals can offer valuable support and guidance. If you're struggling with specific issues, don't hesitate to seek professional help. They can provide tools and strategies to help you cope and connect you with additional resources and support networks.

5) Cultivate online connections

In today's digital age, online communities can also be a valuable source of support. There are numerous forums, social media groups, and online platforms where you can connect with others who share your interests or experiences. While online interactions shouldn't replace face-to-face connections, they can complement your support network and provide additional avenues for support.

6) Be a supportive friend

Building a support network isn't just about receiving support; it's also about giving it. Be there for your friends and family when they need you. Listen to them, offer your help, and show that you care. Being a supportive friend strengthens your relationships and creates a reciprocal support system.

7) Maintain regular communication

Staying in touch with your support network is essential. Make an effort to communicate regularly with the people in your life. This could be through phone calls, text messages, video chats, or in-person meetings. Regular communication helps keep your relationships strong and ensures that you have ongoing support.

8) Create a safe environment

Ensure that your home and social environments are safe and supportive. Surround yourself with people who uplift and encourage you. Avoid toxic relationships and situations that cause unnecessary stress or harm. A positive and supportive environment is crucial for your well-being.

9) Set boundaries

While having a support network is important, it's also essential to set healthy boundaries. Don't be afraid to say no when you need to take care of yourself. Communicate your needs clearly and respectfully, and ensure that your relationships are balanced and mutually supportive.

10) Be patient and persistent

Building a solid support network takes time and effort. Be patient and persistent in connecting with others and building meaningful relationships. Over time, you'll find that having a robust support network can significantly enhance your ability to cope with life's challenges and enjoy a fulfilling and balanced life.

A support network is a cornerstone of ongoing healing and well-being. By nurturing relationships with family and friends, joining support groups, participating in community activities, seeking professional help, cultivating online connections, being a supportive friend, maintaining regular communication, creating a safe environment, setting boundaries, and being patient and persistent, you can build a robust and reliable support network that will support you through life's ups and downs.

11.4 Engage in continuous learning and growth

Engaging in continuous learning and growth is vital to maintaining overall well-being and achieving a fulfilling life. Lifelong learning keeps your mind active and sharp and provides opportunities for personal and professional development. Here's how you can make continuous learning and growth a regular part of your life.

Curiosity is the driving force behind continuous learning. Stay curious about the world, and always be open to new ideas and experiences. This means asking questions, seeking out new knowledge, and being willing to challenge your own beliefs and assumptions. Learning becomes a natural and enjoyable process when you maintain a curious mindset.

Setting specific learning goals can help you stay focused and motivated. Think about what skills or knowledge you want to acquire and set clear, achievable goals. These goals can be short-term, like learning a new recipe, or long-term, like mastering a new language. Write down your goals and create a plan to achieve them. Regularly review and adjust your goals as needed to keep yourself on track.

Reading is one of the easiest and most effective ways to learn. Make reading a daily habit, whether books, articles, or online resources. Choose materials that interest you and challenge your thinking. Reading broadens your perspective and exposes you to new ideas and concepts. If you struggle to find time to read, consider audiobooks or podcasts you can listen to while commuting or exercising.

Formal education isn't the only way to learn. Countless online courses and workshops are available on a wide range of topics. Platforms like

Coursera, Udemy, and Khan Academy offer courses you can take at your own pace. These courses can help you develop new skills, advance your career, or explore exciting topics. Don't be afraid to invest time and sometimes money in your education – it's an investment in yourself.

Learning from others can be incredibly enriching. Seek mentors, join study groups, or participate in online forums and discussion groups. Engaging with others allows you to gain different perspectives and insights. It also provides opportunities for collaborative learning, where you can share your knowledge and learn from the experiences of others. Don't hesitate to ask questions and seek advice from knowledgeable people in the areas you want to know about.

Self-reflection is a powerful tool for continuous learning and growth. Take time to reflect on your experiences, both successes and failures. Consider what you've learned from these experiences and how you can apply those lessons in the future. Journaling can be a helpful practice for self-reflection. By writing down your thoughts and insights, you can track your progress and better understand yourself.

Challenges and obstacles are often the best learning opportunities. When you face difficulties, approach them with a growth mindset. Instead of seeing challenges as setbacks, view them as opportunities to develop new skills and knowledge. Embrace the discomfort of learning something new, and don't be afraid to make mistakes. Each mistake is a valuable lesson that brings you one step closer to your goals.

The world is constantly changing, and staying updated on the latest developments in your field or areas of interest is crucial. Follow news sources, subscribe to industry newsletters, and attend conferences and seminars. Staying informed helps you remain relevant and adaptable in a rapidly changing world. It also ensures that your knowledge and skills are current and applicable.

Make learning a part of your daily routine. This could be as simple as dedicating a few minutes each day to reading, watching educational videos, or practicing a new skill. Integrating learning into your daily life makes it a habit rather than a chore. Over time, these small, consistent efforts increase and lead to significant growth over time.

Remember to celebrate your progress. Acknowledge your achievements and take pride in your efforts. Celebrating milestones, no matter how small keeps you motivated and reinforces the value of continuous learning. It also helps you recognize how far you've come and encourages you to keep pushing forward.

Engaging in continuous learning and growth is essential for personal development and well-being. By staying curious and open-minded, setting learning goals, reading regularly, taking courses, learning from others, practicing self-reflection, embracing challenges, staying updated, integrating learning into your daily routine, and celebrating your progress, you can cultivate a lifelong love of learning that enriches your life and helps you reach your full potential.

11.5 Practicing self-care and self-compassion

Practicing self-care and self-compassion is crucial for maintaining your well-being and emotional health. Self-care involves preserving or improving your health, while self-compassion is about treating yourself with kindness and understanding, especially during difficult times. Here's how you can incorporate these essential practices into your life.

Self-Care: the foundation of well-being

Self-care is taking care of your physical, mental, and emotional health. It's about ensuring you're doing the things that keep you feeling good and functioning well. Here are some key aspects to consider:

Physical self-care

Physical self-care includes all the activities that help you maintain your physical health. This means eating a balanced diet, exercising regularly, and getting enough sleep. Taking care of your body is fundamental because physical health impacts overall well-being.

Healthy eating: focus on eating a variety of nutritious foods. Add fruits, vegetables, whole grains, and lean proteins to your meals. Avoid excessive consumption of processed foods and sugary drinks. Remember, what you eat directly affects your energy levels and feelings.

Regular exercise: aim for at least 30 minutes of moderate exercise most days of the week. Exercise can be anything you enjoy, like walking, jogging, yoga, or dancing. Physical activity helps reduce stress, improve mood, and boost overall health.

Adequate sleep: make sure you're getting enough sleep each night. Adults typically need 7-9 hours of sleep. Establish a bedtime routine to help you unwind and create an environment conducive to sleep, such as keeping your bedroom cool, dark, and quiet.

Mental and emotional self-care

Mental and emotional self-care involves activities that help you manage stress and maintain a positive mindset. This can include hobbies, relaxation techniques, and social activities.

Relaxation techniques: practice relaxation methods like meditation, deep breathing, or mindfulness exercises. These techniques help reduce stress and promote a sense of calm. Taking a few minutes daily to focus on your breath or meditate can make a big difference.

Hobbies and interests: engage in activities you enjoy and that bring you happiness. This could be anything from reading, painting, gardening, or playing a musical instrument. Hobbies provide a mental break and a great way to relax and recharge.

Social connections: A crucial aspect of self-compassion is maintaining healthy relationships with friends and family. These social interactions are not just for emotional support but also to help you feel connected and valued. Make time to connect with loved ones through phone calls, video chats, or in-person meetings, as these interactions are an integral part of practicing self-compassion.

Self-Compassion: being kind to yourself

Self-compassion is a powerful tool that empowers you to treat yourself with the same kindness and care you would offer a friend. It's about acknowledging that everyone makes mistakes and experiences difficulties, and choosing to be gentle with yourself during these times. Here are some ways to harness this power and practice self-compassion:

Mindful self-awareness

Mindful self-awareness is a powerful tool for self-compassion. It's about being present with your feelings and experiences without judgment. By practicing mindful self-awareness, you acknowledge your thoughts and emotions without getting caught up in them. This can help you respond to yourself with kindness and understanding, and ultimately, improve your overall well-being.

Recognize your feelings: when experiencing a complex emotion, take a moment to acknowledge it. Say to yourself, "I'm feeling sad" or "I'm feeling stressed." Simply recognizing your feelings can help you process them more effectively.

Avoid self-criticism: Notice when you're being overly critical of yourself. Instead of harshly judging yourself for mistakes or shortcomings, speak to yourself as you would to a friend. Be supportive and understanding. Remember that being imperfect is okay, and everyone goes through tough times.

Self-kindness and encouragement

Self-kindness involves treating yourself with warmth and encouragement, especially during failure or difficulty. It's about giving yourself the same compassion you would offer someone you care about.

Practice positive self-talk: replace negative self-talk with positive and supportive statements. For example, instead of saying, "I'm not good enough," try saying, "I'm doing my best, and that's enough." Positive self-talk can boost your confidence and help you maintain a positive outlook.

Celebrate your efforts: acknowledge and celebrate your achievements, no matter how small. Give yourself credit for the effort you put in, and recognize your progress. Celebrating your efforts reinforces a positive mindset and encourages you to keep progressing.

Incorporating self-care and self-compassion into your daily routine is not just about improving your overall well-being, it's about finding self-fulfillment. By caring for your physical, mental, and emotional health and treating yourself with kindness and understanding, you create a foundation for a happier and healthier life. Remember, self-care and self-compassion are not selfish—they are essential practices that enable you to be your best self and to support others effectively, and they bring a deep sense of satisfaction and contentment.

11.6 Personal goal setting and achievement

Setting and achieving personal goals is essential to personal growth and development. Whether big or small, goals give you direction, purpose, and motivation to make positive changes in your life. Here are some practical steps to help you set and achieve your goals.

11.6.1 Identifying your values and priorities

Before you can set meaningful goals, you must identify your values and priorities. Your values are the principles or beliefs most important to you, guiding your decisions and actions. Take some time to reflect on what matters most to you in life. Consider your passions, interests, and the person you want to be. Once you clearly understand your values, you can align your goals with them, ensuring that they are meaningful and fulfilling.

Reflect on Your Values: Spend some time thinking about what matters most to you. Consider aspects such as family, career, relationships, health, personal growth, and spirituality. Identify the values that resonate with you the most and prioritize them.

Set Priorities: Determine which areas of your life are most important to you right now. What do you want to focus on and improve? By setting priorities, you can direct your energy and efforts toward the areas that matter most, helping you make progress more effectively.

11.6.2 Setting SMART goals

Once you've identified your values and priorities, it's time to set specific, measurable, achievable, relevant, and time-bound (SMART) goals. SMART goals are clear and actionable, providing a roadmap for success. Here's how to set SMART goals:

Specific: clearly define what you want to achieve. Be specific about the desired outcome and why it's important to you.

Measurable: determine how you will measure your progress and know when you've achieved your goal. Set concrete criteria for success.

Achievable: ensure that your goal is realistic and attainable. Consider your resources, skills, and time frame.

Relevant: ensure your goal aligns with your values, priorities, and long-term objectives. It should be meaningful and pertinent to your overall vision for your life.

Time-Bound: set a deadline for achieving your goal. A specific time frame creates a sense of urgency and helps you stay focused and motivated.

11.6.3 Creating an Action Plan

Once you've defined your SMART goals, it's time to create an action plan outlining the steps you need to take to achieve them. An action plan breaks down your goals into manageable tasks and provides a roadmap for success. Here's how to create an action plan:

Break It Down: divide your goal into smaller, more manageable tasks or milestones. This makes your goal less overwhelming and allows you to track your progress more effectively.

Set Deadlines: assign deadlines to each task to keep yourself accountable and on track. Be realistic about the time required to complete each task.

Identify Resources: determine what resources you need to accomplish your goals, such as time, money, skills, or support from others. Identify any obstacles or challenges you may encounter and plan how to overcome them.

Monitor and Adjust: regularly review your progress and adjust your action plan as needed. Celebrate your successes and learn from any setbacks or obstacles you encounter.

By identifying your values and priorities, setting SMART goals, and creating an action plan, you can effectively set and achieve your personal goals. Remember to stay focused, stay motivated, and stay flexible as you work towards making positive changes in your life. With determination and perseverance, you can turn your dreams into reality and create a fulfilling and meaningful life.

Conclusion

Well, my friend, we've ended our journey together! As we close the final chapter of this book, I want to take a moment to reflect on the importance of what we've discussed and the transformative power of Catholic spirituality in healing our inner wounds.

Throughout these pages, we've delved into the depths of our souls, confronting painful memories and exploring the impact of childhood experiences on our adult lives. We've examined the wounds of rejection, abandonment, and shame, recognizing that these wounds are not just personal but also spiritual.

But amid our pain and brokenness, we've discovered a profound source of healing and hope in Christ's teachings and the Catholic Church's traditions. We've seen how faith, love, and forgiveness can illuminate the path to wholeness, offering comfort to our wounded inner child.

One of the key insights we've gained is the importance of forgiveness— both of others and of ourselves. We've learned that forgiveness is not just about letting go of past hurts but also about reclaiming our power and freedom from the grip of resentment and bitterness. By extending forgiveness to those who have hurt us, we open ourselves to receiving God's healing grace and experiencing the true liberation of our hearts.

Another vital aspect of our journey has been the practice of self-compassion. We've learned that self-compassion is not a sign of weakness but a courageous act of self-love and acceptance. By treating ourselves with kindness and understanding, we create a nurturing environment for our wounded inner child to heal and grow.

But perhaps the most profound realization we've come to is the truth of our identity as beloved children of God. No matter what wounds we carry or mistakes we've made, our Heavenly Father deeply loves and cherishes us. We are worthy, valuable, and deserving of all good things in His eyes. As we embrace this truth, we find the strength and courage to embark on the healing journey with confidence and hope.

As we bring our journey to a close, I want to leave you with a final thought. While our focus has been on healing our inner child, the lessons we've learned and the principles we've explored have broader implications for our lives and our world. In a society that often values success over authenticity and achievement over connection, healing our inner child reminds us of the importance of vulnerability, compassion, and love.

By embracing our woundedness and allowing ourselves to be seen and known, we find healing for ourselves and become agents of healing and transformation in the world around us. As we extend grace and compassion to ourselves and others, we create a ripple effect of healing that reaches far beyond our lives.

So, my friend, as you close the pages of this book and continue on your journey, remember that you are never alone. God walks with you every step of the way, offering His love and grace to guide and sustain you.

Made in United States
Troutdale, OR
07/19/2024